THE ELEMENTARY SCHOOL KIDS'

Book of Lists

from the **KIDS' STUFF** People

Acknowledgment

To Daniel P. Crowe III for creating the division pages.

Library of Congress Catalog Card Number 81-80910
ISBN Number: 0-86530-047-X

To all the kids whose parents and teachers say,
"Go look it up."

To all the parents and teachers who grew up
hearing the same line.

TABLE OF CONTENTS

THINGS (cont.)

STUDY HELPS

YOUR LIST

Dame Judith Anderson	Greta Garbo	Jack Nicholson
Eddie "Rochester" Anderson	Judy Garland	David Niven
Julie Andrews	John Gielgud	Edna Mae Oliver
Alan Arkin	Hermoine Gingold	Maureen O'Sullivan
Gene Autry	Dorothy Gish	Peter O'Toole
Pearl Bailey	Lillian Gish	Al Pacino
Anne Bancroft	Ruth Gordon	Gregory Peck
Talullah Bankhead	Cary Grant	Mary Pickford
Theda Bara	Robert Guillaume	Sidney Poitier
Ethel Barrymore	Alec Guinness	William Powell
John Barrymore	Nell Gwynne	Vincent Price
Lionel Barrymore	Jean Harlow	Basil Rathbone
Warren Beatty	Rex Harrison	Robert Redford
Ingrid Bergman	Sessue Hayakawa	Sir Michael Redgrave
Sarah Bernhardt	Audrey Hepburn	Vanessa Redgrave
Humphrey Bogart	Katharine Hepburn	Sir Ralph Richardson
Ernest Borgnine	Charlton Heston	Jason Robards, Jr.
Charles Boyer	Dustin Hoffman	Paul Robeson
Marlin Brando	Judy Holliday	Bill Robinson
Yul Brenner	Lena Horn	Edward G. Robinson
Richard Burton	Trevor Howard	Esther Rolle
Francis X. Bushman	Walter Huston	Diana Ross
James Cagney	Boris Karloff	Will Sampson
John Carradine	Buster Keaton	Maxmilian Schell
Dianne Carroll	Gene Kelly	Paul Scofield
Lon Chaney	Grace Kelly	George C. Scott
Charlie Chaplin	Burt Lahr	Peter Sellers
Maurice Chevalier	Burt Lancaster	Sarah Siddons
Jill Clayburg	Lillie Langtry	Jay Silverheels
Montgomery Clift	Elsa Lanchester	Dame Edith Sitwell
Claudette Colbert	Charles Laughton	Sissy Spacek
Jackie Coogan	Vivien Leigh	James Stewart
Gary Cooper	Jack Lemmon	Meryl Streep
Joan Crawford	Sophia Loren	Gloria Swanson
Bette Davis	Peter Lorre	Elizabeth Taylor
Doris Day	Myrna Loy	Shirley Temple
Olivia De Havilland	Bela Lugosi	Spencer Tracy
James Dean	Shirley MacClaine	Lana Turner
Marlene Dietrich	Fred MacMurray	Cicely Tyson
Melvyn Douglas	Butterfly McQueen	Peter Ustinov
Faye Dunaway	Jayne Mansfield	Rudolph Valentino
Dame Edith Evans	Chico Marx	Ben Vereen
Douglas Fairbanks	Groucho Marx	Ethel Waters
Alice Faye	Harpo Marx	John Wayne
Stepin Fetchit	David Merrick	Raquel Welch
W. C. Fields	Tom Mix	Orson Welles
Errol Flynn	Marilyn Monroe	Mae West
Henry Fonda	Agnes Moorehead	Billy Dee Williams
Jane Fonda	Zero Mostel	Natalie Wood
Clark Gable	Paul Newman	Joanne Woodward

FAMOUS 𝒜RCHITECTS

Name	Home Country
Alvar Aalto (1898-1976)	Finland
James (1730-1794) & Robert (1728-1792) Adam	England
Dankmar Adler (1844-1900)	Germany/USA
Leone B. Alberti (1404-1472)	Italy
Peter Behrens (1868-1940)	Germany
Giovanni L. Bernini (1598-1680)	Italy
Francesco Borromini (1599-1667)	Italy
Donato Bramante (1444-1514)	Italy
Filippo Brunelleschi (1377-1446)	Italy
Charles Bulfinch (1763-1844)	USA
Daniel H. Burnham (1846-1912)	USA
Peter Dickinson (1925-1961)	Canada
Buckminster Fuller (1895-)	USA
Jacques-Ange Gabriel (1710-1782)	France
Antonio Gaudi (1852-1926)	Spain
Giotto (1266?-1337)	Italy
Walter Gropius (1883-1969)	Germany/USA
Irving Grossman (1926-)	Canada
Richard M. Hunt (1827-1895)	USA
Thomas Jefferson (1743-1826)	USA
William Le Brown Jenney (1832-1907)	USA
Inigo Jones (1573-1652)	England
Benjamin H. Latrobe (1764-1820)	England/USA
Le Corbusier (1887-1965)	Switzerland/France
Sir Edwin L. Lutyens (1869-1944)	England
Francois Mansart (1598-1666)	France
Eric Mendelsohn (1887-1953)	Germany
Michelangelo (1475-1564)	Italy
Ludwig Mies van der Rohe (1886-1969)	Germany/USA
Balthasar Neuman (1687-1753)	Germany
Richard Neutra (1892-1970)	Austria/USA
Oscar Niemeyer (1907-)	Brazil
Andrea Palladio (1508-1580)	Italy
John Parkin (1922-)	Canada
Henry H. Richardson (1838-1886)	USA
Eliel Saarinen (1873-1950)	Finland
Eero Saarinen (1910-1961)	USA
Paolo Soleri (1919-)	Italy
Edward D. Stone (1902-1978)	USA
Louis H. Sullivan (1856-1924)	USA
Ronald Thom (1923-)	Canada
Sir John Vanbrugh (1664-1726)	England
Giorgio Vasari (1511-1574)	Italy
Henry Van DeVelde (1863-1957)	Belgium
Thomas U. Walter (1804-1887)	USA
Stanford White (1853-1906)	USA
Sir Christopher Wren (1632-1723)	England
Frank Lloyd Wright (1869-1959)	USA

FAMOUS ARTISTS AND SELECTED WORKS

AMERICAN

John James Audubon (1780-1850)	*The Birds of America*
George Bellows (1882-1925)	*Lady Jean*
Thomas Hart Benton (1889-1975)	*Roasting Ears*
George Caleb Bingham (1811-1879)	*Fur Traders Descending the Missouri*
Charles Burchfield (1893-1967)	*Promenade*
Alexander Calder (1898-1976)	*Pomegranate* (mobile)
Mary Cassatt (1845-1926)	*The Bath*
John Singleton Copley (1737-1815)	*Mrs. Seymour Fort*
John Steuart Curry (1897-1946)	*The Line Storm*
Arthur Dove (1880-1946)	*Moon*
Marcel Duchamp (1887-1968)	*Nude Descending a Staircase*
Thomas Eakins (1844-1916)	*The Concert Singer*
Lyonel Feininger (1871-1956)	*Gelmeroda*
Morris Graves (1910-)	*Bird Searching*
Winslow Homer (1836-1910)	*Hound and Hunter*
Edward Hopper (1882-1967)	*Gas*
Reginald Marsh (1898-1954)	*Twenty Cent Movie*
Robert Motherwell (1915-)	*Afternoon in Barcelona*
"Grandma" Moses (Anna Mary Robertson) 1860-1961)	*The Harvest*
Georgia O'Keefe (1887-)	*Black Iris*
Charles Willson Peale (1741-1827)	*George Washington*
Jackson Pollock (1912-1956)	*Reflection of the Big Dipper*
Norman Rockwell (1894-1978)	*Saturday Evening Post* covers
Albert Pinkham Ryder (1847-1917)	*The Forest of Arden*
Augustus Saint-Gaudens (1848-1907)	*The Puritan*
John Singer Sargent (1856-1925)	*Madame X*
Ben Shahn (1898-1969)	*Troubled Man*
John Sloan (1871-1951)	*McSorley's Bar*
Gilbert Steuart (1775-1828)	*George Washington*
Andy Warhol (1930-)	*Campbell's Soup*
James Abbot Whistler (1834-1903)	*Whistler's Mother*
Grant Wood (1892-1942)	*American Gothic*
Andrew Wyeth (1917-)	*Treasure Island* illustrations
James Wyeth (1946-)	*J.F.K.*

ANCIENT GREEK — (Sculpture)

Lysippus (c. 400-350 B.C.)	*Apozyomenos*
Myron (mid-5th century B.C.)	*Discus Thrower*
Polykieitos (5th century B.C.)	*Doryphoros*
Praxiteles (4th century B.C.)	*Aphrodite*

BELGIAN

James Ensor (1860-1949)	*Carnival*

(cont.)

DUTCH

George Breitner (1857-1923)	*Brouwersgracht*
Frans Hals (1580-1666)	*The Jester*
Meindert Hobbema (1638-1709)	*Avenue at Middleharms*
Pieter De Hooch (1629-1677)	*Interior of a Dutch House*
Asger Jorn (1914-)	*Letter to My Son*
Johan Jongkind (1819-1891)	*In Holland*
Willem De Kooning (1904-)	*Woman I*
Piet Mondrian (1872-1944)	*Composition with Red, Yellow, and Blue*
Van Rijn Rembrandt (1606-1669)	*The Sampling Officials of the Drapers' Guild*
Jacob Van Ruisdael (1628-1682)	*Wheat Fields*
Jan Steen (1626-1679)	*The Eve of St. Nicholas*
Jan Vermeer (1632-1675)	*The Cook*

ENGLISH

William Blake (1757-1827)	*Book of Job*
Thomas Chippendale (1718-1779)	Furniture
John Constable (1776-1837)	*The Haywain*
Thomas Gainsborough (1727-1788)	*Blue Boy*
William Hogarth (1697-1764)	*The Graham Children*
Sir Henry Raeburn (1756-1823)	*Boy with Rabbit*
Sir Joshua Reynolds (1723-1792)	*Dr. Johnson*
Dante Gabriel Rosetti (1828-1882)	*Dante's Dream*
Graham Sutherland (1903-)	*Le petite Afrique III*
Joseph Mallord Turner (1775-1851)	*The Fighting Temeraire*

FLEMISH

Hieronymous Bosch (c. 1450-1516)	*Garden of Wordly Delights*
Pieter Breughel the Elder (1525-1569)	*Children's Games*
Jan Van Eyck (1385?-1441)	*John Arnolfini and His Wife*
Hans Memling (1430?-1494)	*Madonna and Child*
Peter Paul Rubens (1577-1640)	*The Garden of Love*
Claus Slutter (1375-1400)	*Well of Moses*
Anthony Van Dyck (1599-1641)	*Children of Charles I*
Goger Van Der Weyden (1399-1464)	*Portrait of a Lady*

FRENCH

Jean Arp (1887-1966)	*Die Nabelfalasche*
Pierre Bonnard (1867-1947)	*Nude Taking a Bath*
Georges Braque (1882-1963)	*Guitar, Fruit and Pitcher*
Paul Cézanne (1839-1906)	*Mardi Gras*
Jean-Baptiste Simeon Chardin (1699-1779)	*The Blessing*
Jean Baptiste Corot (1796-1875)	*View of Rome*
Gustave Courbet (1819-1877)	*My Studio*
Honore Daumier (1808-1879)	*The Washwoman*

FRENCH (cont.)

Jacques Louis David (1748-1825)	*Oath of the Horatii*
Edgar Degas (1834-1917)	*Rehearsal of the Ballet on the Stage*
Eugene Delacroix (1798-1863)	*Liberty Leading the People*
Robert Delaunay (1885-1941)	*Circular Forms*
Jean Fouquet (1415-1480)	*St. Margaret*
Jean Honore Fragonard (1732-1806)	*Storming the Citadel*
Paul Gauguin (1848-1903)	*A Sunday Afternoon*
Marc Chagall (1887-)	*The Violinist*
Jean Auguste Ingres (1780-1867)	*Mademoiselle Rivière*
Frank Kupka (1871-1957)	*Architectural Study III*
Fernand Léger (1881-1955)	*Contrast of Forms*
Claude Lorrain (1600-1682)	*The Ford*
Edouard Manet (1832-1883)	*Peonies*
Henri Matisse (1869-1954)	*The Hindu Pose*
Amadeo Modigliani (1884-1920)	*Madam Pompadour*
Claude Monet (1840-1926)	*Water Lilies*
Pablo Picasso (1881-1973)	*Guernica*
Nicolas Poussin (1594-1665)	*The Funeral of Phocion*
Odilon Redon (1840-1916)	*The Chariot of Phaéton*
Pierre Renoir (1841-1919)	*Luncheon of the Boating Party*
Auguste Rodin (1840-1917)	*The Kiss* (sculpture)
Henri Rousseau (1844-1910)	*The Dream*
Georges Seurat (1859-1891)	*La Grande Jatte*
Henri De Toulouse-Lautrec (1864-1901)	*At the Moulin Rouge*
Maurice Utrillo (1883-1955)	*Sacré-Coeur*
Vincent Van Gogh (1853-1890)	*Self Portrait*

GERMAN

Max Beckmann (1884-1950)	*Self-Portrait with Saxophone*
Lucas Cranach (1472-1553)	*Nymph of the Spring*
Albrecht Dürer (1471-1528)	*Hare*
Max Ernst (1891-1976)	*Landscape*
Antoine Jean Grosz (1771-1835)	*Homage to Oskar Panizza*
Mathias Grünewald (1480?-1530?)	*Holy Night*
Hans Holbein (1497-1543)	*The Ambassadors*
Wassily Kandinsky (1866-1944)	*Arrows*
Adolf Menzel (1815-1905)	*Staircase with Night Lighting*
Lasar Segall (1890-1957)	*Brazilian Landscape*

ISRAELI

Mordechai Ardon (1896-)	*The House of the Maggid*

ITALIAN - Sienese School

Duccio di Buoninsegna (1255-1319)	*Temptation of Christ*
Simone Martini (1284-1344)	*Annunciation*
Sassetta (1392-1451)	*Journey of the Magi*

(cont.)

ITALIAN - Paduan School
Andrea Mantegna (1431-1506)   *The Adoration of the Shepherds*

ITALIAN - Florentine School
Fra Angelico (1387-1455)   *The Annunciation*
Sandro Botticelli (1444-1510)   *Primavera*
Andrea Del Castagno (1390-1457)   *The Last Supper*
Benvenuto Cellini (1500-1571)   *The Rospigliosi Cup*
Donatello (1386-1466)   *David*
Lorenzo Ghiberti (1378-1455)   *Gates of Paradise*
Giotto Di Bondone (1266?-1337)   *The Flight into Egypt*
Leonardo Da Vinci (1452-1519)   *Mona Lisa*
Fra Fiiippo Lippi (1406-1469)   *Virgin Adoring the Child*
Tommaso Masaccio (1401-1428)   *The Tribute Money*
Michelangelo Buonarroti (1475-1564)   Sistine Chapel ceiling
Antonio Pollaiuolo (1432-1498)   *Hercules and Antaeus* (bronze)
Paolo Uccello (1396-1477)   *Battle of San Romano*
Andrea Del Verrocchio (1435-1488)   *Colleoni* (bronze)

ITALIAN - Umbrian School
Piero Della Francesca (1410-1492)   *History of the True Cross*
Sanzio Raphael (1483-1520)   *Sistine Madonna*
Luca Signorelli (1450-1523)   *The End of the World*

ITALIAN - Venetian School
Giovanni Bellini (1429-1516)   *Agony in the Garden*
Giorgio Giorgione (1476-1510)   *Fete Champetre*
Francesco Guardi (1712-1793)   *The Piazzetta, Venice*
Antonello Da Messina (1430?-1479?)   *St. Jerome*
Jacopo Robusti Tintoretto (1518-1594)   *The Last Supper*
Tiziano Titian (1477-1576)   *Assumption of the Virgin*
Paolo Veronese (1528-1588)   *Feast in the House of Levi*

ITALIAN - Roman-Parma School
Michelangelo Merisi Da Caravaggio
   (1573-1610)   *Conversion of St. Paul*
Lorenzo Bernini (1598-1680)   *Apollo and Daphne* (bronze)

ITALIAN FUTURISTS
Umberto Boccioni (1882-1916)   *Unique Forms of Continuity in Space*
Carlo Carra (1881-1966)   *The Funeral of the Anarchist Galli*
Gino Severini (1883-1966)   *Dynamic Hieroglyphic of the Bal*
                                                *   Tabarin*

JAPANESE-AMERICAN
Isamu Noguchi (1904-1971)   *Tabel*

────────────────── (cont.) ──

FAMOUS ARTISTS AND SELECTED WORKS (cont.)

MEXICAN

Jose Clemente Orozco (1883-1949)	*The Menaces*
Diego Rivera (1886-1957)	*Man and Machinery*

NORWEGIAN

Edvard Munch (1863-1944)	*The Cry*

SPANISH

Salvador Dali (1904-)	*Persistence of Memory*
El Greco (1541?-1614)	*Toledo in a Storm*
Francisco Goya (1746-1828)	*Naked Maja*
Joan Miró (1893-)	*Bullfight*
Diego Velasquez (1599-1666)	*Maids In Waiting*
Jose Ribera (1591-1652)	*Assumption of Mary Magdalene*

SWISS

Alberto Giacometti (1901-1966)	*Figure in a Box*

SWISS-GERMAN

Paul Klee (1879-1940)	*Sinbad the Sailor*

U. S. ASTRONAUTS

Crew	Date	Mission	Special Significance
Alan Shepard, Jr.	5/5/61	Mercury-Redstone 3	First American in space
Virgil Grissom	7/21/61	Mercury-Redstone 4	
John Glenn, Jr.	2/20/62	Mercury-Atlas 6	First American in orbit
Scott Carpenter	5/24/62	Mercury-Atlas 7	
Walter Schirra, Jr.	10/3/62	Mercury-Atlas 8	
Gordon Cooper	5/15 to 5/16/63	Mercury-Atlas 9	
Virgil Grissom John Young	3/23/65	Gemini-Titan 3	First manned spacecraft to change orbital path
James McDivitt Edward White, II	6/3 to 6/7/65	Gemini-Titan 4	White, first man to walk in space
Gordon Cooper, Jr. Charles Conrad, Jr.	8/21 to 8/29/65	Gemini-Titan 5	
Frank Borman James Lovell, Jr.	12/4 to 12/18/65	Gemini-Titan 7	Longest duration Gemini flight

(cont.)

Crew	Date	Mission	Special Significance
Walter Schirra, Jr. Thomas Stafford	12/15 to 12/16/65	Gemini-Titan 6-A	First space rendezvous (with Gemini 7)
Neil Armstrong David Scott	3/16 to 3/17/66	Gemini-Titan 8	First docking of one spacecraft with another
John Young Michael Collins	7/18 to 7/21/66	Gemini-Titan 10	Rendezvous with Gemini 8
Charles Conrad, Jr. Richard Gordon, Jr.	9/12 to 9/15/66	Gemini-Titan 11	
James Lovell, Jr. Edwin Aldrin, Jr.	11/11 to 11/15/66	Gemini-Titan 12	Record 5½ hrs. extra-vehicular activity
Walter Schirra, Jr. Donn Eisele Walter Cunningham	10/11 to 10/22/68	Apollo-Saturn 7	First manned flight of Apollo Command Module
Frank Borman James A. Lovell, Jr. William Anders	12/21 to 12/27/68	Apollo-Saturn 8	First flight to Moon; televised to earth views of lunar surface
James McDivitt David Scott Russell Schweickart	3/3 to 3/13/69	Apollo-Saturn 9	First manned flight of lunar module
Thomas Stafford Eugene Cernan John Young	5/18 to 5/26/69	Apollo-Saturn 10	First lunar module to orbit the moon
Neil Armstrong Edwin Aldrin, Jr. Michael Collins	7/16 to 7/24/69	Apollo-Saturn 11	First lunar landing by Armstrong and Aldrin; lunar stay 21 h 36 m
Charles Conrad, Jr. Richard Gordon Alan Bean	11/14 to 11/24/69	Apollo-Saturn 12	Second lunar landing; lunar stay 31 h 31 m
James Lovell, Jr. Fred Haise, Jr. John Swigart, Jr.	4/11 to 4/17/70	Apollo-Saturn 13	Aborted; returned safely
Alan Shepard, Jr. Stuart Roosa Edgar Mitchell	1/31 to 2/9/71	Apollo-Saturn 14	Third lunar landing; lunar stay 33 h 31 m
David Scott Alfred Worden James Irwin	7/26 to 8/7/71	Apollo-Saturn 15	First lunar rover used. First deep space walk. Lunar stay 66 h 55 m
Charles Duke, Jr. Thomas Mattingly John Young	4/16 to 4/27/72	Apollo-Saturn 16	Fifth lunar landing; lunar stay 71 h 2 m

Crew	Date	Mission	Special Significance
Eugene Cernan Ronald Evans Harrison Schmitt	12/7 to 12/19/72	Apollo-Saturn 17	Record lunar stay of 75 h
Charles Conrad, Jr. Joseph Kerwin Paul Weitz	5/25 to 6/22/73	Skylab 2	First American manned orbiting space station
Alan Bean Jack Lousma Owen Garriott	7/28 to 9/25/73	Skylab 3	
Gerald Carr Edward Gibson William Pogue	11/16/73 to 2/8/74	Skylab 4	Spacewalk record: 7 hr 1 m. Final Skylab Mission
Vance Brand Thomas Stafford Donald Slayton	7/15 to 7/24/75	Apollo 18	US-USSR joint flight. Crews linked up in space.

FAMOUS *A*THLETES

MEN ATHLETES

Name	Sport	Country or Team
Hank Aaron	Baseball	Atlanta Braves (USA)
Muhammed Ali	Boxing	USA
Mario Andretti	Auto Racing	USA
Eddie Arcaro	Horse Racing	USA
Bjorn Borg	Tennis	Sweden
Jim Brown	Football	Syracuse (USA)
Don Carter	Bowling	USA
Jimmy Connors	Tennis	USA
James J. Corbett	Boxing	USA
Robin Cousins	Figure Skating	Great Britain
Jack Dempsey	Boxing	USA
Klaus Dibiasi	Diving	Italy
A J Foyt	Auto Racing	USA
Eric Heiden	Speed Skating	USA
Ben Hogan	Golf	USA
Bobby Hull	Hockey	Winnipeg (Canada)
Bruce Jenner	Track	USA
Bobby Jones	Golf	USA
Joe Louis	Boxing	USA
Jerry Lucas	Basketball	Ohio State (USA)
Mickey Mantle	Baseball	New York Yankees (USA)
Willie Mays	Baseball	New York Giants (USA)
George Mikan	Basketball	De Paul (USA)
Stan Musial	Baseball	St. Louis Cardinals (USA)
Jack Nicklaus	Golf	USA
Jesse Owens	Track	USA
Arnold Palmer	Golf	USA
Richard Petty	Auto Racing	USA
Jackie Robinson	Baseball	Brooklyn Dodgers (USA)
Pete Rose	Baseball	Philadelphia Phillies (USA)
Bill Russell	Basketball	San Francisco (USA)
Vladimir Salnikov	Swimming	USSR
Ard Schenk	Speed Skating	Netherlands
Willie Shoemaker	Horse Racing	USA
O J Simpson	Football	So. California (USA)
Peter Snell	Track	New Zealand
Mark Spitz	Swimming	USA
Amos Alonzo Stagg	Football	Yale (USA)
Jackie Stewart	Auto Racing	Scotland
John L. Sullivan	Boxing	USA
Jim Thorpe	Football	Carlisle (USA)
Dick Weber	Bowling	USA
Ted Williams	Baseball	Boston Red Sox (USA)
John Wooden	Basketball	Purdue (USA)

WOMEN ATHLETES

Name	Sport	Country
Melissa Belote	Swimming	USA
Barbara Ann Cochran	Skiing	USA
Nadia Comaneci	Gymnastics	Rumania
Mary Decker	Track	USA
Gertrude Ederle	Swimming	USA
Peggy Fleming	Figure Skating	USA
Althea Gibson	Tennis	USA
Evonne Goolagong	Tennis	Australia
Janet Guthrey	Auto Racing	USA
Anne Henning	Speed Skating	USA
Sonja Henie	Figure Skating	Norway
Billie Jean King	Tennis	USA
Micki King	Diving	USA
Olga Korbut	Gymnastics	USSR
Kathy Kusner	Horse Racing	USA
Chris Evert-Lloyd	Tennis	USA
Shirley Muldowney	Auto Racing	USA
Cathy Rigby	Gymnastics	USA
Wilma Rudolph	Track	USA
Eleanora Sears	Tennis/Sailing	USA
Teresa Shank	Basketball	USA
Wyomia Tyus Simburg	Track	USA
Robyn Smith	Horse Racing	USA
Ludmila Tatova	Skating	USSR
Babe Didrikson Zaharias	Golf/Basketball/ Baseball/Track	USA

SOME FAMOUS AUTHORS

Aesop (6th century B.C.)   Greek
Aesop's Fables
Louisa May Alcott (1832-1888)   American
Little Men
Jane Austin (1775-1817)   English
Pride and Prejudice
Francis Bacon (1561-1626)   English
The Advancement of Learning
James Baldwin (1924-   )   American
Nobody Knows My Name
Charles Pierre Baudelaire (1821-1867)   French
Les Fleurs du mal (Flowers of Evil)
William Blake (1757-1827)   English
Scngs of Innocence
Robert Burns (1759-1796)   Scotch
"Auld Lang Syne"
Joseph Conrad (1857-1924)   English
Lord Jim
James Fenimore Cooper (1789-1851)   American
The Last of the Mohicans
Stephen Crane (1871-1900)   American
The Red Badge of Courage
Dante (1265-1321)   Italian
Divine Comedy
Daniel Defoe (1660-1731)   English
Robinson Crusoe
Charles Dickens (1812-1870)   English
Tale of Two Cities
Emily Dickinson (1830-1886)   American
Poems
Fedor Dostoevsky (1821-1881)   Russian
Crime and Punishment
Sir Arthur Conan Doyle (1859-1930)   English
The Complete Sherlock Holmes
Alexandre Dumas (1802-1870)   French
The Count of Monte Cristo
Daphne du Maurier (1907-   )   English
Rebecca
Lawrence Durrell (1912-   )   English
Balthazar
T. S. Eliot (1888-1965)   English
The Waste Land
William Faulkner (1897-1962)   American
The Sound and the Fury
Edna Ferber (1887-1968)   American
Showboat
Eleanor Farjeon (1881-1965)   English
Poems for Children
Henry Fielding (1707-1754)   English
The History of Tom Jones
Erle S. Gardner (1889-1970)   American
Murder Up My Sleeve

Jakob Grimm (1785-1863)	German
German Grammar	
Wilhelm Grimm (1786-1859)	German
Fairy Tales	
Thomas Hardy (1840-1928)	English
Tess of the D'Urbervilles	
Nathaniel Hawthorne (1804-1864)	American
The House of the Seven Gables	
Oliver Wendell Holmes (1809-1894)	American
The Autocrat of the Breakfast Table	
Homer (850?B.C.)	Greek
The Illiad	
Aldous Huxley (1894-1963)	English
Brave New World	
Washington Irving (1783-1859)	American
The Legend of Sleepy Hollow	
Henry James (1843-1916)	American
Portrait of a Lady	
Samuel Johnson (1709-1784)	English
Dictionary of the English Language	
James Joyce (1882-1941)	Irish
Ulysses	
John Keats (1795-1821)	English
"Endymion: A Poetic Romance"	
Rudyard Kipling (1865-1936)	English
The Jungle Book	
Ray Lawler (1921-)	Australian
Summer of the Seventeenth Doll	
Henry Lawson (1867-1922)	Australian
While the Billy Boils	
Sinclair Lewis (1885-1951)	American
Babbitt	
Anne Morrow Lindbergh (1906-)	American
Gift from the Sea	
Hugh Lofting (1886-1947)	English
The Voyages of Dr. Dolittle	
Henry Wadsworth Longfellow (1807-1882)	American
Evangeline	
Hugh MacLennan (1907-)	Canadian
Return of the Sphinx	
Norman Mailer (1923-)	American
The Naked and the Dead	
Sir Thomas Malory (15th Century)	English
Morte d'Arthur	
Wm. Somerset Maugham (1874-1965)	English
Of Human Bondage	
Herman Melville (1819-1891)	American
Moby Dick	
James Michener (1907-)	American
Hawaii	
Edna St. Vincent Millay (1892-1950)	American
A Few Figs from Thistles	

———— (cont.) ————

Arthur Miller (1915-   )   American
The Crucible
John Milton (1608-1674)   English
Paradise Lost
Ogden Nash (1902-1971)   American
Good Intentions
Sean O'Casey (1880-1964)   Irish
The Plough and the Stars
Eugene O'Neill (1888-1953)   American
The Iceman Cometh
Thomas Paine (1737-1809)   English/American
Common Sense
Sir Gilbert Parker (1862-1932)   Canadian
The Power and the Glory
Alan Stewart Paton (1903-   )   South African
Cry, the Beloved Country
Edgar Allan Poe (1809-1849)   American
The Raven and Other Poems
Alexander Pope (1688-1744)   English
The Rape of the Lock
Wm. Sydney Porter (O.Henry) (1862-1910)   American
Rolling Stones
Beatrix Potter (1866-1943)   English
Tale of Peter Rabbit
Edwin John Pratt (1883-1964)   Canadian
Towards the Last Spike
Marcel Proust (1871-1922)   French
Remembrance of Things Past
Henry H. Richardson (1870-1946)   Australian
The Getting of Wisdom
James Whitcomb Riley (1849-1916)   American
Green Fields and Running Brooks
Sir Charles Roberts (1860-1943)   Canadian
In the Morning of Time
Christina Rossetti (1830-1894)   English
Sing Song
Damon Runyon (1900-1946)   American
Guys and Dolls
Jerome David Salinger (1919-   )   American
Franny and Zooey
George Sand (1804-1876)   French
Lélia
Carl Sandburg (1878-1967)   American
The People, Yes
William Saroyan (1908-   )   American
The Human Comedy
Sir Walter Scott (1771-1832)   Scotch
Ivanhoe
Robert William Service (1874-1958)   Canadian
Ballads of a Bohemian

William Shakespeare (1564-1616)	English
Hamlet	
George Bernard Shaw (1856-1950)	English (Irish-born)
Pygmalion	
Mary Shelley (1797-1851)	English
Frankenstein	
Upton Sinclair (1878-1968)	American
Roman Holiday	
Aleksandr Solzhenitsyn (1918-)	Russian
The Gulag Archipelago	
John E. Steinbeck (1902-1968)	American
The Grapes of Wrath	
Harriet Beecher Stowe (1811-1896)	American
Uncle Tom's Cabin	
Jonathan Swift (1667-1745)	English
Gulliver's Travels	
Alfred Tennyson (1809-1892)	English
Idylls of the King	
Dylan Thomas (1914-1953)	English
The World I Breathe	
Henry D. Thoreau (1817-1862)	American
Walden: or, Life in the Woods	
James Thurber (1894-1961)	American
My World — And Welcome to It!	
Alexis de Tocqueville (1805-1859)	French
Democracy in America	
Count Nikolaevich Tolstoy (1828-1910)	Russian
War and Peace	
John Updike (1932-)	American
Bech: a Book	
Virgil (70-19 B.C.)	Ancient Roman
The Aeneid	
Jules Verne (1828-1905)	French
20,000 Leagues Under the Sea	
Voltaire (1694-1778)	French
Candide	
Robert Penn Warren (1905-)	American
All the King's Men	
H. G. Wells (1866-1946)	English
The War of the Worlds	
Patrick White (1912-)	Australian
The Living and the Dead	
Walt Whitman (1819-1892)	American
Leaves of Grass	
William Wordsworth (1770-1850)	English
The Recluse	
William Butler Yeats (1865-1939)	Irish
The Winding Stair	

KIDS'S STUFF LIST OF *A*UTHORS OF GREAT CHILDREN'S BOOKS

Authors	Selected Works
Alcott, Louisa May	Little Women
Andersen, Hans Christian	Andersen's Fairy Tales
Barrie, James	Peter Pan
Carroll, Lewis	Alice's Adventures in Wonderland
Cather, Willa	My Antonia
Collodi, Carlo	The Adventures of Pinocchio
cummings, e.e.	Tulips and Chimneys
DeBrunhoff, Jean	The Story of Babar
Dickens, Charles	David Copperfield
Grahame, Kenneth	The Wind in the Willows
Grimm, Jakob and Wilhelm	Grimms' Fairy Tales
Halliburton, Richard	The Flying Carpet
Henry, O.	Works of O. Henry
Keats, Ezra Jack	The Snowy Day
Kipling, Rudyard	Just So Stories
Lear, Edward	The Complete Nonsense Book
L'Engle, Madeline	A Wrinkle in Time
Longfellow, Henry W.	Ballads and Other Poems
McCloskey, Robert	Time of Wonder
Milne, A. A.	When We Were Very Young
Nash, Ogden	Good Intentions
Rawlings, Marjorie	The Yearling
Riley, James Whitcomb	The Old Swimmin' Hole
Rossetti, Christina	Sing Song
Sandburg, Carl	Wind Song
Sendak, Maurice	Where the Wild Things Are
Steele, William O.	The Perilous Road
Stevenson, Robert Louis	Treasure Island
Teasdale, Sara	Stars Tonight
Tolkien, J. R. R.	The Hobbit
Twain, Mark	The Adventures of Tom Sawyer
Verne, Jules	20,000 Leagues Under the Sea
White, E. B.	The Trumpet of the Swan
Wilde, Oscar	The Selfish Giant

SOME FAVORITE COMPOSERS

John Antill (1904-)	Australian
Louis "Satchmo" Armstrong (1900-1971)	American
Johann Sebastian Bach (1685-1750)	German
Bela Bartok (1881-1945)	Hungarian
Ludwig Van Beethoven (1770-1827)	German
Aleksandr Borodin (1834-1887)	Russian
Johannes Brahms (1833-1897)	German
Irving Berlin (1888-)	American
Leonard Bernstein (1918-)	American
Pablo Casals (1876-1973)	Spanish
Frederic Chopin (1810-1849)	Polish
Aaron Copeland (1900-)	American
Claude Debussy (1862-1918)	French
Anton Dvorak (1841-1904)	Czech
Edward K. "Duke" Ellington (1899-1974)	American
George Gershwin (1898-1937)	American
Eduard Greig (1843-1907)	Norwegian
Ferde Grofe (1892-1972)	American
Oscar Hammerstein (1895-1960)	American
George Frederick Handel (1685-1759)	British (German-born)
Joseph Haydn (1732-1809)	Austrian
Alfred Hill (1870-1960)	Australian
Ernst Hoffman (1776-1822)	German
Scott Joplin (1868-1917)	American
Jerome D. Kern (1885-1945)	American
Ernesto Lecuona (1896-)	Cuban
Franz Liszt (1811-1886)	Hungarian
Frederick Loewe (1904-)	American (Austrian-born)
Gustav Mahler (1860-1911)	Austrian
Jakob Mendelssohn (1809-1847)	German
Wolfgang Mozart (1756-1791)	Austrian
Modest Mussorgsky (1835-1881)	Russian
Cole Porter (1891-1964)	American
Sergei Prokofiev (1891-1953)	Russian
Giacomo Puccini (1858-1924)	Italian
Sergei Rachmaninoff (1873-1943)	Russian
Maurice Ravel (1875-1937)	French
Nikolai Rimski-Korsakov (1844-1908)	Russian
Richard Rodgers (1902-)	American
Sigmund Romberg (1887-1951)	American (Hungarian-born)
Robert Schumann (1810-1856)	German
Andrés Segovia (1893-)	Spanish
Dimitri Shostakovich (1906-1975)	Russian
John Philip Sousa (1854-1932)	American
Richard Strauss (1864-1949)	German
Igor Stravinsky (1882-1971)	American (Russian-born)
Petr Tchaikovsky (1840-1893)	Russian
Richard Wagner (1813-1883)	German

PROMINENT **H**ANDICAPPED PEOPLE

Person	Contribution	Handicap
Ludwig van Beethoven	great German composer	deafness
Sarah Bernhardt	actress	leg amputated in 1915
Rocky Bleier	NFL star running back	serious leg injuries in Vietnam
Louis Braille	developed a code of dots, now known as the Braille Alphabet, to help blind people read	blindness
Elizabeth Barrett Browning	English Victorian Poet	injured spine in fall
Roy Campanella	shared his courage to ''live again'' after tragic end to baseball career	injured in auto accident
Thomas Alva Edison	inventor and technologist	deafness
Francisco Goya	Spanish painter	deafness
Ben Hogan	American golfer	overcame injuries in car wreck after having been told he would never walk again
Helen Keller	made millions realize deaf-mutes failed to develop speech because they couldn't hear	blind-deaf-mute
John Milton	English poet who wrote one of world's greatest epics, *Paradise Lost*	blindness
Itzhak Perlman	concert violinist	polio victim
Franklin Delano Roosevelt	President of U.S. (elected 4 times — 1933-1945)	polio victim
Wilma Rudolph	Olympic Gold Medal Winner	polio victim
Henri de Toulouse-Lautrec	French painter	broke both legs at 14 which caused him to stop growing (became dwarfish)

MAJOR CONTRIBUTORS TO WORLD HEALTH

Person	Contribution
Aesculapius	Earliest physician in Greek history
Christiaan Barnard	Performed first heart transplant
Celsus	Wrote earliest medical book
Edwin Chadwick	Early campaigner for sewers, garbage disposal, pure water and clean streets
Madame Marie and Pierre Curie	Discovered radium
H. Dreser	Introduced aspirin to medicine
Philip Drinker	Invented the iron lung
Christiaan Eijkman and Frederick Hopkins	Discovered existence of vitamins
Sir Alexander Fleming	Discovered penicillin
Sigmund Freud	Founder of the study of psychoanalysis
Galen	Emphasized importance of study of anatomy
Galileo Galilei	Made first thermometer
Stephen Hales	Made the first demonstration of blood pressure
William Harvey	Developed the theory of circulation of blood
Hippocrates	Greek physician who developed the medical Hippocratic Oath
Dr. Edward Jenner	First innoculation against smallpox—beginning of vaccinations
Robert Koch	Established bacteriology
Karl Landsteiner	Demonstrated different blood types
Antoine Lavoisier	Studied the chemistry of breathing and the need for oxygen
Anton von Leeuwenhoek	Dutch naturalist who was a pioneer in microscopy
Lord Lister	Developed first antiseptic system for surgery
Crawford Long and Wm. Morton	First to use ether in surgery as anesthetic
Richard Lower	Made the first successful blood transfusion
William and Charles Mayo	Established center to deal with every kind of medical problem
Gregor J. Mendel	Laid foundation for study of heredity (genetics)
Franz Mesmer	First used hypnotism in medicine
Florence Nightingale	Founded nursing profession
Ambroise Paré	Helped make surgery respected form of treatment
Louis Pasteur	Made discoveries in immunology and microbiology leading to pasteurization and rabies treatment
Ivan Pavlov	Studied the effects of conditioned reflexes
Philippe Pinel	First reformer for mental health
Walter Reed	Identified mosquito as carrier of malaria
Wilhelm Roentgen	Discovered x-rays for medical use
Albert B. Sabin	Developed oral vaccine against polio
Jonas Salk	Introduced first successful polio vaccine
Ignaz Semmelweis	Emphasized cleanliness in surgery and hospitals
Abbé Sicard	Made a code of manual gestures for the deaf
René Theophile and Hyacinthe Laënnec	Invented the stethoscope
Andreas Vesalius	"Father of anatomy"

Player	School	Position	Year
Jay Berwanger	Chicago	HB	1935
Larry Kelley	Yale	E	1936
Clinton Frank	Yale	QB	1937
David O'Brien	Texas Christian	QB	1938
Nile Kinnick	Iowa	QB	1939
Tom Harmon	Michigan	HB	1940
Bruce Smith	Minnesota	HB	1941
Frank Sinkwich	Georgia	HB	1942
Angelo Bertelli	Notre Dame	QB	1943
Leslie Horvath	Ohio State	QB	1944
Felix Blanchard	Army	FB	1945
Glenn Davis	Army	HB	1946
John Lujack	Notre Dame	QB	1947
Doak Walker	SMU	HB	1948
Leon Hart	Notre Dame	E	1949
Vic Janowicz	Ohio State	HB	1950
Richard Kazmaier	Princeton	HB	1951
Billy Vessels	Oklahoma	HB	1952
John Lattner	Notre Dame	HB	1953
Alan Ameche	Wisconsin	FB	1954
Howard Cassady	Ohio State	HB	1955
Paul Hornung	Notre Dame	QB	1956
John Crow	Texas A & M	HB	1957
Pete Dawkins	Army	HB	1958
Billy Cannon	Louisiana State	HB	1959
Joe Bellino	Navy	HB	1960
Ernest Davis	Syracuse	HB	1961
Terry Baker	Oregon State	QB	1962
Roger Staubach	Navy	QB	1963
John Huarte	Notre Dame	QB	1964
Mike Garrett	USC	HB	1965
Steve Spurrier	Florida	QB	1966
Gary Beban	UCLA	QB	1967
O.J. Simpson	USC	RB	1968
Steve Owens	Oklahoma	RB	1969
Jim Plunkett	Stanford	QB	1970
Pat Sullivan	Auburn	QB	1971
Johnny Rodgers	Nebraska	RB-R	1972
John Cappelletti	Penn State	RB	1973
Archie Griffin	Ohio State	RB	1974
Archie Griffin	Ohio State	RB	1975
Tony Dorsett	Pittsburgh	RB	1976
Earl Campbell	Texas	RB	1977
Billy Sims	Oklahoma	RB	1978
Charles White	USC	RB	1979
George Rogers	South Carolina	RB	1980

NOBEL PEACE PRIZE WINNERS

Year	Recipient	Reason
1979	Mother Theresa of Calcutta	Work among the poor, destitute and sick of Calcutta for more than 30 years.
1978	Anwar Sadat (Egypt) Menachem Begin (Israel)	Efforts to bring about settlement of Arab-Israeli conflict
1977	Amnesty International	Work to help political prisoners
1976	Mairead Corrigan, Betty Williams (N. Ireland)	Organizing movements to end Protestant-Catholic fighting in N. Ireland
1975	Andrei Sakharov (USSR)	Efforts in support of peace and in opposition to violence and brutality
1974	Eisaku Sato (Japan)	Efforts to improve international relations and stop spread of nuclear weapons
	Sean MacBride (Ireland)	Work to guarantee human rights through International Law
1973	Henry Kissinger (USA) Le Duc Tho (N. Vietnam) [declined]	Negotiating Vietnam War cease-fire agreement
1971	Willy Brandt (W. Germany)	Efforts to improve relations between Communist and non-Communist nations
1970	Norman E. Borlaug (USA)	For role in developing high-yield grains that increased food production in developing countries
1969	International Labor Organization	Efforts to improve working conditions
1968	Rene Cassin (France)	Furthering cause of human rights
1965	United Nations Children's Fund (UNICEF)	Aid to children
1964	Martin Luther King, Jr. (USA)	Leading black struggle for equality in U.S. by non-violent means
1963	International Red Cross; League of Red Cross Societies	Humanitarian work
1962	Linus C. Pauling (USA)	Trying to effect a ban on nuclear weapons
1961	Dag Hammarskjöld (Sweden)	Efforts to bring peace to the Congo
1960	Albert J. Luthuli (South Africa)	Peaceful campaign against racial restrictions in South Africa
1959	Philip J. Noel-Baker (Britain)	Work in promoting peace and disarmament
1958	Georges Pire (Belgium)	Work in resettling displaced persons
1957	Lester B. Pearson (Canada)	Organizing UN force in Egypt
1954	Office of UN, High Commissioner for Refugees	Protection for millions of refugees and seeking solutions to their problems

(cont.)

Year	Recipient	Reason
1953	George C. Marshall (USA)	Promoting peace through European Recovery Program
1952	Albert Schweitzer (France)	Humanitarian work in Africa
1951	Leon Jouhaux (France)	Working to organize national and international labor unions
1950	Ralph Bunche (USA)	UN mediator in Palestine in 1948 and 1949
1949	Lord John Boyd Orr of Brechin Mearns (Britian)	Directing U.N. Food and Agriculture Organization
1947	Friends Service Council (Britain) American Friends Service Commission	Humanitarian work
1946	Emily Balch (USA)	Work with Women's International League for Peace and Freedom
	John R. Mott (USA)	YMCA work — aiding displaced persons
1945	Cordell Hull (USA)	Peace efforts as Secy. of State
1944	International Red Cross	Relief work during World War II
1938	Nansen International Office for Refugees	Directing relief work among refugees
1937	Viscount Cecil of Chelwood (Britain)	Promoting League of Nations; working with peace movements
1936	Carlos de Saavedra Lamas (Argentina)	Negotiating peace settlement between Bolivia and Paraguay in Chaco War
1935	Carl von Ossietzky (Germany)	Promoting world disarmament
1934	Arthur Henderson (Britain)	President of World Disarmament Conference
1933	Sir Norman Angell (Britain)	Work with Royal Institute of Inter. Affairs, League of Nations and National Peace Council
1931	Jane Addams (USA)	Work with Women's Inter. League for Peace and Freedom
	Nicholas Murray Butler (USA)	Work with Carnegie Endowment for International Peace
1930	Nathan Söderblom (Sweden)	Writing and working for peace
1929	Frank Kellogg (USA)	Negotiating Kellogg-Briand Pact
1927	Ferdinand E. Buisson (France)	Pres. of League of Human Rights
	Ludwig Quidde (Germany)	Writings on peace
1926	Aristide Briand (France)	Forming Locarno Peace Pact
	Gustav Stresemann (Germany)	Persuading Germans to accept plans for reparations
1925	Sir J. Austen Chamberlain (Britain)	Helping work out Locarno Peace Pact
	Charles G. Dawes (USA)	Originating plan for payment of German reparations
1922	Fridtjof Nansen (Norway)	Relief work among Russian prisoners of war and famine in areas of Russia

Year	Recipient	Reason
1921	Karl H. Branting (Sweden)	Promoting social reforms in Sweden
	Christian L. Lange (Norway)	Secy. Gen. of the International Parliamentary Union
1920	Leon V. A. Bourgeois (France)	Pres. of Council of League of Nations
1919	Woodrow Wilson (USA)	Attempting just settlement of W.W.I. Advocating League of Nations
1917	International Red Cross	Relief work during World War I
1913	Henri La Fontaine (Belgium)	President of International Peace Bureau
1912	Elihu Root (USA)	Settling problem of Japanese immigration to California and organizing Central American Peace Conference
1911	Tobias M. C. Asser (Dutch)	Organizing conference on International Law
	Alfred H. Fried (Austria)	Writings on peace
1910	Permanent International Peace Bureau	Promoting international arbitration
1909	Auguste M. F. Beernaert (Belgium)	Work on Permanent Court of Arbitration
	Paul H. B. B. d'Estourmelles de Constant (France)	Founding French Parliamentary Arbitration Committee and League of International Conciliation
1908	Klas P. Arnoldson (Sweden)	Founding Swedish Society for Peace and Arbitration
	Frederick Bajer (Denmark)	Work on International Peace Bureau
1907	Ernesto T. Moneta (Italy)	President of Lombard League for Peace
	Louise Renault (France)	Organizing international peace conference
1906	Theodore Roosevelt (USA)	Negotiating peace in Russo-Japanese War
1905	Baroness Bertha von Suttner (Austria)	Pacifism — Founding Austrian Peace Society
1904	Institute of International Law	Studies on laws of neutrality
1903	Sir William R. Cremer (Britain)	Founder and secretary of International Arbitration League
1902	Elie Ducommun (Switzerland)	Honorary Sec'y., International Peace Bureau
	Charles A. Gobat (Switzerland)	Administrator, Inter-Parliamentary Union
1901	Jean H. Dunant (Switzerland)	Founding Red Cross. Originating Geneva Conference
	Frederic Passy (France)	Founding French Peace Society

FAMOUS U.S. FIGURES

BENJAMIN FRANKLIN (1706-1790) — American statesman, author, scientist and inventor.

GEORGE WASHINGTON (1732-1799) — Commander-in-Chief of the Colonial Army during the Revolutionary War. First President of the United States.

THOMAS JEFFERSON (1743-1826) — Author of the Declaration of Independence. Third President of the United States.

ELIZABETH (MOTHER) SETON (1774-1821) — Established parochial school education in the United States.

JOHN JAMES AUDUBON (1785-1851) — Artist and naturalist who painted hundreds of definitive pictures of birds in their natural surroundings.

HORACE MANN (1796-1859) — Attorney, teacher, lecturer and crusader for public education.

JEFFERSON DAVIS (1808-1889) — President of the Confederate States of America.

ABRAHAM LINCOLN (1809-1865) — President of the United States during Civil War. Made the Emancipation Proclamation. Credited with preserving the union of the United States.

CLARA BARTON (1821-1912) — Nurse during the Civil War. Founded and served as president of the American Red Cross.

SAMUEL CLEMENS (1835-1910) — Author of many colorful stories about everyday American life, written under the pen name of Mark Twain.

THOMAS ALVA EDISON (1847-1931) — American inventor who held over 1,000 patents, including the incandescent electric lamp and the phonograph.

ALEXANDER GRAHAM BELL (1847-1922) — American inventor who patented the first telephone.

LUTHER BURBANK (1849-1926) — Naturalist who created hundreds of new varieties of plants by grafting a shoot of one plant to another.

SAMUEL GOMPERS (1850-1924) — Labor leader; founder and president of the AFL.

WALTER REED (1851-1902) — Army doctor who did definitive research on yellow fever.

BOOKER T. WASHINGTON (1856-1915) — Lecturer, teacher, college president and educator who supported quality education for blacks.

THEODORE ROOSEVELT (1858-1919) — Leader of volunteer soldier group during the Spanish-American War. President of the U.S. Supported the building of the Panama Canal.

———(cont.)———

HENRY FORD (1863-1947) — American auto maker; developed the first popular low-priced automobile.

ALBERT EINSTEIN (1879-1955) — Theoretical physicist noted for the development of the theory of relativity.

HELEN KELLER (1880-1968) — Crusader for better treatment of handicapped people.

FRANKLIN DELANO ROOSEVELT (1882-1945) — Only U.S. President to be elected to four terms of office. Creator of the New Deal. Served as president during the Great Depression and into World War II.

MARGARET MEAD (1901-1978) — Brought the study of cultural anthropology forward as an important addition to the world's knowledge.

JOHN F. KENNEDY (1917-1963) — War hero and 35th President of the United States. Served during the Cuban Missile Crisis and was assassinated in Dallas in 1963.

MARTIN LUTHER KING (1929-1968) — Civil Rights leader who won the Nobel Peace Prize in 1964, and was assassinated in Memphis in 1968.

U.S. PRESIDENTS

	Name	Term of Office	Party	Home State
1.	George Washington	1789-1797	Federalist	Virginia
2.	John Adams	1797-1801	Federalist	Massachusetts
3.	Thomas Jefferson	1801-1809	Rep.-Dem.	Virginia
4.	James Madison	1809-1817	Rep.-Dem.	Virginia
5.	James Monroe	1817-1825	Rep.-Dem.	Virginia
6.	John Quincy Adams	1825-1829	Rep.-Dem.	Massachusetts
7.	Andrew Jackson	1829-1837	Democrat	S. Carolina
8.	Martin Van Buren	1837-1841	Democrat	New York
9.	William Harrison (tnc)	1841	Whig	Virginia
10.	John Tyler	1841-1845	Democrat	Virginia
11.	James K. Polk	1845-1849	Democrat	N. Carolina
12.	Zachary Taylor (tnc)	1849-1850	Whig	Virginia
13.	Millard Fillmore	1850-1853	Whig	New York
14.	Franklin Pierce	1853-1857	Democrat	New Hampshire
15.	James Buchanan	1857-1861	Democrat	Pennsylvania
16.	Abraham Lincoln (tnc)	1861-1865	Republican	Kentucky
17.	Andrew Johnson	1865-1869	Republican	N. Carolina

(cont.)

Name	Term of Office	Party	Home State
18. Ulysses S. Grant	1869-1877	Republican	Ohio
19. Rutherford B. Hayes	1877-1881	Republican	Ohio
20. James A. Garfield (tnc)	1881	Republican	Ohio
21. Chester A. Arthur	1881-1885	Republican	Vermont
22. Grover Cleveland	1885-1889	Democrat	New Jersey
23. Benjamin Harrison	1889-1893	Republican	Ohio
24. Grover Cleveland	1893-1897	Democrat	New Jersey
25. William McKinley (tnc)	1897-1901	Republican	Ohio
26. Theodore Roosevelt	1901-1909	Republican	New York
27. William Taft	1909-1913	Republican	Ohio
28. Woodrow Wilson	1913-1921	Democrat	Virginia
29. Warren G. Harding (tnc)	1921-1923	Republican	Ohio
30. Calvin Coolidge	1923-1929	Republican	Vermont
31. Herbert Hoover	1929-1933	Republican	Iowa
32. Franklin D. Roosevelt (tnc)	1933-1945	Democrat	New York
33. Harry S. Truman	1945-1953	Democrat	Missouri
34. Dwight D. Eisenhower	1953-1961	Republican	Texas
35. John F. Kennedy (tnc)	1961-1963	Democrat	Massachusetts
36. Lyndon B. Johnson	1963-1968	Democrat	Texas
37. Richard M. Nixon (tnc)	1968-1974	Republican	California
38. Gerald R. Ford	1974-1977	Republican	Nebraska
39. James Earl Carter, Jr.	1977-1981	Democrat	Georgia
40. Ronald W. Reagan	1981-	Republican	California

tnc — term not completed.

FAMOUS **W**ORLD FIGURES

Dean Acheson (1893-1971)	American statesman
Samuel Adams (1722-1803)	American statesman
Konrad Adenauer (1876-1967)	Chancellor of West Germany
Alfred Adler (1870-1937)	Viennese psychologist
Aga Khan III (1877-1957)	Head of Ismailian Muslims
Alaric (370?-410)	Gothic king and conqueror
John Alden (1599?-1687)	English-American settler
Alexander the Great (356 B.C.-323 B.C.)	Greek conqueror
Samuel Alexander (1859-1938)	Australian philosopher
Alfred the Great (849-899)	King of West Saxons
Dame Judith Anderson (1898-)	Australian actress
Anders Angstrom (1814-1874)	Swedish astronomer
Marc Antony (83?-30 B.C.)	Roman orator and soldier
Johnny Appleseed (John Chapman) (1774-1845)	American pioneer and folk hero
St. Thomas Aquinas (1225-1274)	Italian theologian
Aristotle (384-322 B.C.)	Greek philosopher
Louis Armstrong (''Satchmo'') (1900-1971)	American jazz musician
Benedict Arnold (1741-1801)	American general and traitor
John Jacob Astor (1763-1848)	German-American financier
Clement Attlee (1883-1967)	English labor leader
Gaius Octavius Augustus (63 B.C.-A.D. 14)	First Roman emperor
Francis Bacon (1561-1626)	English philosopher
Pearl Mae Bailey (1918-)	American singer
Nuñez de Balboa (1475-1519)	Spanish explorer
Bernard Baruch (1870-1965)	American businessman and statesman
William Beaumont (1785-1853)	American surgeon
St. Thomas á Becket (1118?-1170)	English archbishop
Louis Begin (1840-1925)	Canadian cardinal
Alexander Graham Bell (1819-1905)	Scottish-American inventor
Richard B. Bennett (1870-1947)	Canadian statesman
Sarah Bernhardt (1845-1923)	World-renowned actress
Otto van bram Bismarck (1815-1890)	First chancellor of German empire
Louis Blériot (1872-1936)	French engineer
William Bligh (1754-1817)	English naval officer
Niels Bohr (1885-1962)	Danish physicist
Simon Bolivar (1783-1830)	South American revolutionary leader
Napoleon Bonaparte (1769-1821)	French emperor
Louis Botha (1862-1919)	South African soldier-statesman
Nathaniel Bowditch (1773-1838)	American mathematician
Sir John S. Bradbury (1872-1950)	English treasury official
Omar Bradley (1893-)	American general
Tycho Brahe (1546-1601)	Danish astronomer
Louis Braille (1809-1852)	French teacher of the blind
Wernher von Braun (1912-1977)	German-American engineer

(cont.)

Leonid Ilyich Brezhnev (1906-)	Russian politician
Sir Alan F. Brooke (1883-1963)	British soldier
John Brown (1800-1859)	American abolitionist
Marcus Junius Brutus (85?-42 B.C.)	Roman politician
William Jennings Bryan (1860-1925)	American politician
Luther Burbank (1849-1926)	American horticulturist
Warren Earl Burger (1907-)	Chief Justice of the American Supreme Court
Martha Jane Burke ("Calamity Jane") (1852-1903)	American frontierswoman
Sir Macfarlane Burnet (1899-)	Australian physician
Ambrose Everett Burnside (1824-1881)	American general
Richard E. Byrd (1888-1957)	American polar explorer
John Cabot (1450-1498)	Discovered continent of North America for England
Julius Caesar (100 B.C.-44 B.C.)	Roman general, statesman and author
John Calvin (1509-1564)	French theologian
Andrew Carnegie (1835-1919)	Scottish-American industrialist and humanitarian
George Cartier (1814-1873)	Canadian statesman
Jacques Cartier (1491-1557)	French navigator and explorer
Edmund Cartwright (1743-1823)	English inventor
Enrico Caruso (1873-1921)	Italian tenor
George Washington Carver (1864-1943)	American botanist
Casanova (1725-1798)	Italian adventurer
Fidel Castro (1927-)	Cuban premier
Catherine the Great (1729-1796)	Empress of Russia
Anders Celsius (1701-1744)	Swedish astronomer
Samuel de Champlain (1567?-1635)	Founder of Quebec
Prince Charles (1948-)	Prince of Wales
Claire Chennault (1890-1958)	American general
Chiang Kaishek (1887-1975)	President of China
Winston Churchill (1874-1965)	British statesman and prime minister
Cicero (106-43 B.C.)	Roman statesman and orator
El Cid (1040?-1099)	Spanish soldier and hero
George Rogers Clark (1752-1818)	American soldier and frontiersman
Henry Clay (1777-1852)	American statesman
Eldridge Cleaver (1935-)	Black American leader
Cleopatra (69-30 B.C.)	Queen of Egypt
Cochise (1812-1874)	Apache Indian chief
Christopher Columbus (1451-1506)	Italian navigator
Confucius (551-479 B.C.)	Chinese philosopher
Constantine the Great (280?-337)	Roman emperor
James Cook (1728-1779)	English navigator and explorer
Nicolaus Copernicus (1473-1543)	Polish astronomer
Lord Cornwallis (1738-1805)	British general
Francisco Coronado (1510-1554)	Spanish explorer
Hernando Cortes (1485-1547)	Spanish explorer
Jacques Cousteau (1910-)	French marine explorer
Crazy Horse (1849-1877)	Sioux chief

"Davy" Crockett (1786-1836)	American frontiersman
Oliver Cromwell (1599-1658)	Lord Protector of England
Marie Curie (1867-1934)	Polish-French chemist
Glen Curtis (1878-1930)	American aviator and inventor
George Custer (1839-1876)	American general
Cyrano de Bergerac (1619-1655)	French poet-soldier
Cyrus the Great (600-529 B.C.)	King of Persia
Gottlieb Daimler (1834-1900)	German auto manufacturer
Virginia Dare (1587-?)	First English child born in America
Clarence Darrow (1857-1938)	American lawyer and social reformer
Charles Darwin (1809-1882)	English naturalist who advanced the theory of evolution
Jefferson Davis (1808-1889)	American military and political statesman; President of the Confederate States of America
Moshe Dayan (1915-)	Israeli statesman
Eugene Debs (1855-1926)	American socialist
John Deere (1804-1886)	American inventor
Lee DeForest (1873-1961)	American inventor
Charles de Gaulle (1890-1970)	French general, statesman and president
Cecil B. DeMille (1881-1959)	American film producer
Democritus (5th Century B.C.)	Greek philosopher
Demosthenes (385-322 B.C.)	Greek philosopher
Rene Descartes (1596-1650)	French mathematician
Hernando de Soto (1500-1542)	Spanish explorer
Eamon DeValera (1882-1975)	Irish politician
John Dewey (1859-1952)	American educator
Bartholomeu Diaz (1450-1500)	Portugese navigator
Porfirio Diaz (1830-1915)	Mexican general and president
Rudolf Diesel (1858-1913)	German engineer
Everett McKinley Dirksen (1896-1969)	American politician
Walter (Walt) Disney (1901-1966)	American cartoonist
Benjamin Disraeli (1804-1881)	English politician
James Doolittle (1896-)	American aviator
Christian Doppler (1803-1853)	Austrian physicist
Stephen A. Douglas (1813-1861)	American politician
Frederick Douglass (1817-1895)	American abolitionist
Sir Francis Drake (1540-1596)	English sailor
John Foster Dulles (1888-1959)	American Secretary of State
Isadora Duncan (1878-1927)	American dancer
E. I. DuPont (1771-1834)	American industrialist
Francois Duvalier (1907-1971)	Haitian dictator
Amelia Earhart (1898-1937)	American aviator
Wyatt Earp (1848-1929)	American lawman
George Eastman (1858-1932)	American inventor
Duke of Edinburgh, Philip (1921-)	English consort to Elizabeth II
Edward, Duke of Windsor (1894-1972)	English king who abdicated
Edward, The Black Prince (1330-1376)	Prince of Wales
Jonathan Edwards (1703-1758)	American theologian
Paul Ehrlich (1854-1915)	German bacteriologist

(cont.)

Albert Einstein (1879-1955)	German-American physicist
Elizabeth I (1533-1603)	Queen of England and Ireland
Elizabeth II (1926-)	Queen of England and Northern Ireland
Ralph Waldo Emerson (1803-1882)	American essayist and poet
Eric the Red (10th Century)	Norwegian navigator; discovered Greenland
Leif Ericson (10th Century)	Norwegian explorer who discovered Vinland (probably coast of North America)
G. D. Fahrenheit (1686-1736)	German physicist
Michael Faraday (1791-1867)	English chemist
David Farragut (1801-1870)	American admiral
Farouk I (1920-1965)	King of Egypt
Guy Fawkes (1570-1606)	English conspirator
Ferdinand V (1452-1516)	Founder of Spanish monarchy
Enrico Fermi (1901-1954)	Italian-American physicist
Alexander Fleming (1881-1955)	British scientist
Henry Ford (1863-1947)	American auto manufacturer
St. Francis of Assisi (1182-1226)	Italian friar
Francisco Franco (1892-1975)	Spanish dictator
Benjamin Franklin (1706-1790)	American statesman and inventor
Frederick the Great (1712-1786)	Prussian king
Sigmund Freud (1856-1939)	Austrian psychologist
Milton Friedman (1912-)	American economist
Martin Frobisher (1535-1594)	English explorer
Comte de Frontenac (Louis de Buade) (1620-1698)	French colonial governor of Canada
Robert Fulton (1765-1815)	American inventor
Yuri Gagarin (1934-1968)	Soviet cosmonaut, first man to orbit the earth in space
John Kenneth Galbraith (1908-)	Canadian-American economist
Galileo Galilei (1564-1642)	Italian astronomer
Indira Gandhi (1917-)	Indian prime minister
Mahatma Gandhi (1869-1948)	Hindu nationalist and spiritual leader
Giuseppe Garibaldi (1807-1882)	Italian patriot
Gautama Buddha (563-483 B.C.)	Founder of Buddhism
Genghis Khan (1162-1227)	Mongol conqueror
George III (1738-1820)	King of England during American Revolution
Geronimo (1829-1909)	Apache chief
Giscard d'Estaing (1926-)	French president
William Gladstone (1809-1898)	British politician
Robert Goddard (1882-1945)	American physicist
George W. Goethals (1858-1928)	Dutch-born American engineer; led the building of the Panama Canal
Samuel Gompers (1850-1924)	American labor leader
Jakob Grimm (1785-1863)	German folklorist

Wilhelm Grimm (1786-1859)	German folklorist
Andre Gromyko (1909-)	Russian diplomat
Johann Gutenberg (1400-1468)	German inventor of movable type
Nathan Hale (1755-1776)	American patriot
Alexander Hamilton (1755-1804)	American statesman
Dag Hammarskjöld (1905-1961)	Swedish diplomat; U.N. Secretary-General
John Hancock (1737-1793)	First signer of the American Declaration of Independence
Hannibal (247-183 B.C.)	Carthaginian general
Warren Hastings (1732-1818)	English statesman
Henry II (1133-1189)	King of England; house of Anjou
Henry VIII (1491-1547)	King of England; house of Tudor
Patrick Henry (1736-1799)	American Revolutionary leader
Sir William Herschel (1792-1871)	English astronomer
Gerhard Herzberg (1904-)	German-Canadian physicist
Hippocrates (460?-377? B.C.)	Greek physician; called the "father of medicine"
Hirohito (1901-)	Emperor of Japan
Adolf Hitler (1889-1945)	German führer
Ho Chi Minh (1890-1969)	President of North Vietnam
John Edgar Hoover (1895-1972)	American F.B.I. director
Julia Howe (1819-1910)	American feminist and pacifist
Henry Hudson (? -1611)	English navigator and explorer
William Morris Hughes (1864-1952)	Australian statesman
Cordell Hull (1871-1955)	American statesman
Hubert H. Humphrey (1911-1978)	American politician
Hussein I (1935-)	King of Jordan
Isabella I (1451-1504)	Queen of Castile; aided Columbus
Ivan III, the Great (1440-1505)	Grand duke of Russia
Ivan IV, the Terrible (1530-1584)	First czar of Russia
Jesse James (1847-1882)	American outlaw
Jesus of Nazareth (4? B.C.-A.D. 29?)	Founder of Christianity
Joan of Arc (1412-1431)	French national heroine
Louis Joliet (or Jolliet) (1645-1700)	French-Canadian explorer
Juan Carlos (1938-)	King of Spain
Benito Pablo Juárez (1806-1872)	President of Mexico
Henry John Kaiser (1882-1967)	American industrialist
Kamehameha the Great (1758?-1819)	King of Hawaii
Estes Kefauver (1903-1963)	American politician
Helen A. Keller (1880-1968)	American deaf and blind lecturer
Robert F. Kennedy (1925-1968)	American politician
Elizabeth Kenny (1886-1952)	Australian nurse
Charles F. Kettering (1876-1958)	American engineer and inventor
Frances Scott Key (1779-1843)	American lawyer and author of "The Star-Spangled Banner"
Nikita Khrushchev (1894-1971)	Premier of Soviet Union
Captain William Kidd (1645?-1701)	Scottish pirate
Martin Luther King (1929-1968)	American Civil Rights leader; winner of the Nobel Peace Prize; assassinated
Henry Kissinger (1923-)	American statesman
Kublai Khan (1216-1294)	Founder of Mongol dynasty in China

(cont.)

Marquis de Lafayette (1757-1834)	French military and political leader; commanded American troops during the Revolution
Lillie Langtry (1853-1929)	British actress
Sieur de La Salle (1643-1687)	Explorer in America
Sir William Laurier (1841-1919)	Canadian statesman
Robert E. Lee (1807-1870)	Commander-in-Chief of the Confederate Army during the Civil War
Vladimir Ilyich Lenin (1870-1942)	Russian Communist leader
Willard Frank Libby (1908-)	American chemist
Lydia Liliuokalani (1838-1917)	Queen of Hawaiian Islands
Jenny Lind (1820-1887)	Swedish soprano
Charles A. Lindbergh (1902-1974)	American aviator
Joseph Lister (1827-1912)	English surgeon
David Livingstone (1813-1873)	Scottish explorer in Africa
John Locke (1632-1704)	English philosopher
Henry Cabot Lodge (1902-)	American diplomat
José Lopez Portillo (1920-)	President of Mexico
Martin Luther (1483-1546)	German Reformation leader
Douglas MacArthur (1880-1964)	American general
James MacDonald (1815-1891)	Canadian statesman
Niccolò Machiavelli (1469-1527)	Italian statesman
Ferdinand Magellan (1480?-1521)	Portugese navigator
Malcolm X (1925-1965)	American Civil Rights leader
Horace Mann (1796-1859)	American educator
Mao Tes-tung (1893-1976)	Chinese Communist leader
Marie Antoinette (1755-1793)	French queen; beheaded during the French Revolution
Jacques Marquette (1637-1675)	Jesuit explorer in America
John Marshall (1755-1835)	American jurist
Karl Marx (1818-1883)	German philosopher; founder of world Communism
Mary Tudor ("Bloody Mary") (1516-1558)	Queen of England
Mary Stuart, Queen of Scots (1542-1587)	Abdicated; beheaded by Elizabeth I
Maximilian (1832-1867)	Emperor of Mexico
Charles H. Mayo (1865-1930)	American surgeon; co-founder of the Mayo Clinic
William J. Mayo (1861-1939)	American surgeon; co-founder of the Mayo Clinic
William H. McGuffey (1800-1873)	American educator
Andrew George McNaughton (1887-1966)	Canadian diplomat
Margaret Mead (1901-1978)	American anthropologist
George Meany (1894-1980)	American labor leader
Golda Meir (1898-1978)	Prime Minister of Israel
Dame Nellie Melba (1861-1931)	Australian soprano
Maria Montessori (1870-1952)	Italian educator
Montezuma II (1480?-1520)	Last Aztec emperor of Mexico

Samuel B. Morse (1791-1872)	Inventor of the telegraph and creator of the Morse code
Moses (c.1200 B.C.)	Hebrew prophet
Muhammad (570-632)	Arab prophet
Benito Mussolini (1883-1945)	Italian Fascist premier
Nero (37-68)	Roman emperor
Sir Isaac Newton (1642-1727)	English mathematician
Nicholas II (1868-1918)	Last Czar of Russia
Florence Nightingale (1820-1910)	English nurse and hospital reformer
Vaslav Nijinsky (1890-1950)	Russian dancer and choreographer
Ovid (43 B.C.-A.D.17?)	Roman poet
George H. Palmer (1842-1933)	American educator
Sir Henry Parkes (1815-1896)	Australian statesman
George Patton (1885-1945)	American general
Ivan Pavlov (1849-1936)	Russian physiologist
Anna Pavlova (1885-1931)	Russian ballerina
George Peabody (1795-1869)	American philanthropist
William Penn (1644-1718)	English Quaker leader; proprietor of Pennsylvania
Juan Perón (1895-1974)	President of Argentina
Oliver Perry (1785-1819)	American naval officer
Jean Piaget (1896-)	Swiss psychologist
Plato (427?-347 B.C.)	Greek philosopher
Pocahontas (1595?-1617)	American Indian princess
Marco Polo (1254?-1324?)	Italian traveler
Ponce de Leon (1460?-1521)	Spanish explorer
Pontiac (1720?-1769)	Ottawa Indian chief
Emily Post (1873-1960)	American columnist
Protagoras (481?-411 B.C.)	Greek philosopher
Joseph Pulitzer (1847-1911)	Hungarian-born American journalist
George M. Pullman (1831-1897)	American inventor
Sir Walter Raleigh (1552?-1618)	English navigator, colonist and author
Walter Reuther (1907-1970)	American labor leader
Paul Revere (1735-1818)	American patriot
Richard the Lionhearted (1157-1199)	King of England
John D. Rockefeller (1839-1937)	American industrialist and philanthropist
Erwin Rommel (1891-1944)	German field marshal
Betsy Ross (1752-1836)	Maker of the first American flag
Artur Rubinstein (1886-)	Polish-born American concert pianist
George "Babe" Ruth (1895-1948)	American baseball player
Anwar el Sadat (1918-)	President of Egypt
Jonas Salk (1914-)	American physician
Albert Schweitzer (1875-1965)	French philosopher; winner of the Nobel Peace Prize
Alan Shepard (1923-)	American astronaut
Philip Henry Sheridan (1831-1888)	American general

——— (cont.) ———

William Tecumseh Sherman (1820-1892)	American (Union) general during the Civil War
Igor Sikorsky (1889-1972)	Russian-born American aeronautical engineer
B. Frederick Skinner (1904-)	American psychologist
John Smith (1580-1631)	English colonist; explorer of America; author
Joseph Smith (1805-1844)	American founder of Mormon Church
Joan Sutherland (1926-)	Australian soprano
Benjamin Spock (1903-)	American physician
Joseph Stalin (1879-1953)	Russian Communist leader
Miles Standish (1584?-1656)	English colonist in America
Tecumseh (1768-1813)	Shawnee Indian chief
Tutankhamen (late 14th Century B.C.)	Boy king of Egypt
Cornelius Vanderbilt (1794-1877)	American financier and philanthropist
Amerigo Vespucci (1454-1512)	Italian navigator; named America
Queen Victoria (1819-1901)	Queen of England for 64 years
Booker T. Washington (1856-1915)	Black American educator
Daniel Webster (1782-1852)	American orator
Noah Webster (1758-1843)	American lexicographer
Duke of Wellington (1769-1852)	British statesman
Eli Whitney (1765-1825)	American inventor
Roy Wilkins (1901-)	American Civil Rights leader
William the Conqueror (1027-1087)	King of England
Orville Wright (1871-1948)	Co-constructor and pilot of the first heavier-than-air craft
Wilbur Wright (1867-1912)	Co-constructor and pilot of the first heavier-than-air craft
Brigham Young (1801-1877)	American Mormon leader
Count Ferdinand von Zeppelin (1838-1917)	German general
Florenz Ziegfeld (1869-1932)	American theatrical producer

WORLD FAMOUS PAIRS

Antony & Cleopatra
George Burns & Gracie Allen
Miss Piggy & Kermit the Frog
Launcelot & Guinevere
Archie & Edith Bunker
Peter Pumpkin & his wife
David & Bathsheba
Roy Rogers & Dale Evans
Punch & Judy
Helen of Troy & Paris
Ralph & Alice Cramden
Lerner & Lowe
Beatrice & Benedict
Rhett Butler & Scarlet O'Hara
Blondie & Dagwood
Humphrey Bogart & Lauren Bacall
Robert & Elizabeth Barrett Browning
Adam & Eve
Bonnie & Clyde
Cupid & Psyche
Don Quixote & Dulcinea
Czar Nicholas & Alexandra
Clark Gable & Carole Lombard
Laura & Dr. Zhivago
Greta Garbo & John Gilbert
Charles & Mary Lamb
Fred Astaire & Ginger Rogers
Damon & Phythias
Tweedledum & Tweedledee
Dido & Aeneas
Abbott & Costello
Orpheus & Eurydice
Darby & Joan
Venus & Adonis
Wilma & Fred Flintstone
Laurel & Hardy
Cheech & Chong
Hansel & Gretel

Beauty & the Beast
Tristram & Iseult
Ozzie & Harriet
Lady & the Tramp
Romeo & Juliet
Superman & Lois Lane
Boris & Natasha
Solomon & the Queen of Sheba
Tarzan & Jane
Jack & Jill
Pocahontas & John Smith
Winnie-the-Pooh & Christopher Robin
Lucy & Desi
Oberon & Titania
The Owl & the Pussycat
Rocky & Bullwinkle
Eliza Doolittle & Henry Higgins
Spencer Tracy & Katharine Hepburn
Marie Antoinette & Louis XVI
Napoleon & Josephine
Robin Hood & Maid Marion
W. C. Fields & Mae West
Otello & Desdemoma
Abelard & Heloise
Rogers & Hammerstein
Gilbert & Sullivan
Castor & Pollux
Vernon & Irene Castle
David & Jonathan
Nelson Eddy & Jeanette MacDonald
Odysseus & Penelope
Katherine & Petruchio
Romulus & Remus
Kaufmann & Hart
Amos & Andy
Sylvester & Tweety

Year	Winner	Loser	Games
1903	Boston (AL)	Pittsburgh (NL)	5-3
1905	New York (NL)	Philadelphia (AL)	4-1
1906	Chicago (AL)	Chicago (NL)	4-2
1907	Chicago (NL)	Detroit (AL)	4-0-1
1908	Chicago (NL)	Detroit (AL)	4-1
1909	Pittsburgh (NL)	Detroit (AL)	4-3
1910	Philadelphia (AL)	Chicago (NL)	4-1
1911	Philadelphia (AL)	New York (NL)	4-2
1912	Boston (AL)	New York (NL)	4-3-1
1913	Philadelphia (AL)	New York (NL)	4-1
1914	Boston (NL)	Philadelphia (AL)	4-0
1915	Boston (AL)	Philadelphia (NL)	4-1
1916	Boston (AL)	Brooklyn (NL)	4-1
1917	Chicago (AL)	New York (NL)	4-2
1918	Boston (AL)	Chicago (NL)	4-2
1919	Cincinnati (NL)	Chicago (AL)	5-3
1920	Cleveland (AL)	Brooklyn (NL)	5-2
1921	New York (NL)	New York (AL)	5-2
1922	New York (NL)	New York (AL)	4-0-1
1923	New York (AL)	New York (NL)	4-2
1924	Washington (AL)	New York (NL)	4-3
1925	Pittsburgh (NL)	Washington (AL)	4-3
1926	St. Louis (NL)	New York (AL)	4-3
1927	New York (AL)	Pittsburgh (NL)	4-0
1928	New York (AL)	St. Louis (NL)	4-0
1929	Philadelphia (AL)	Chicago (NL)	4-1
1930	Philadelphia (AL)	St. Louis (NL)	4-2
1931	St. Louis (NL)	Philadelphia (AL)	4-3
1932	New York (AL)	Chicago (NL)	4-0
1933	New York (NL)	Washington (AL)	4-1
1934	St. Louis (NL)	Detroit (AL)	4-3
1935	Detroit (AL)	Chicago (NL)	4-2
1936	New York (AL)	New York (NL)	4-2
1937	New York (AL)	New York (NL)	4-1
1938	New York (AL)	Chicago (NL)	4-0
1939	New York (AL)	Cincinnati (NL)	4-0
1940	Cincinnati (NL)	Detroit (AL)	4-3
1941	New York (AL)	Brooklyn (NL)	4-1
1942	St. Louis (NL)	New York (AL)	4-1
1943	New York (AL)	St. Louis (NL)	4-1

Year	Winner	Loser	Games
1944	St. Louis (NL)	St. Louis (AL)	4-2
1945	Detroit (AL)	Chicago (NL)	4-3
1946	St. Louis (NL)	Boston (AL)	4-3
1947	New York (AL)	Brooklyn (NL)	4-3
1948	Cleveland (AL)	Boston (NL)	4-2
1949	New York (AL)	Brooklyn (NL)	4-1
1950	New York (AL)	Philadelphia (NL)	4-0
1951	New York (AL)	New York (NL)	4-2
1952	New York (AL)	Brooklyn (NL)	4-3
1953	New York (AL)	Brooklyn (NL)	4-2
1954	New York (AL)	Cleveland (NL)	4-0
1955	Brooklyn (NL)	New York (AL)	4-3
1956	New York (AL)	Brooklyn (NL)	4-3
1957	Milwaukee (NL)	New York (AL)	4-3
1958	New York (AL)	Milwaukee (NL)	4-3
1959	Los Angeles (NL)	Chicago (AL)	4-2
1960	Pittsburgh (NL)	New York (AL)	4-3
1961	New York (AL)	Cincinnati (NL)	4-1
1962	New York (AL)	San Francisco (NL)	4-3
1963	Los Angeles (NL)	New York (AL)	4-0
1964	St. Louis (NL)	New York (AL)	4-3
1965	Los Angeles (NL)	Minnesota (AL)	4-3
1966	Baltimore (AL)	Los Angeles (NL)	4-0
1967	St. Louis (NL)	Boston (AL)	4-3
1968	Detroit (AL)	St. Louis (NL)	4-3
1969	New York (NL)	Baltimore (AL)	4-1
1970	Baltimore (AL)	Cincinnati (NL)	4-1
1971	Pittsburgh (NL)	Baltimore (AL)	4-3
1972	Oakland (AL)	Cincinnati (NL)	4-3
1973	Oakland (AL)	New York (NL)	4-3
1974	Oakland (AL)	Los Angeles (NL)	4-1
1975	Cincinnati (NL)	Boston (AL)	4-3
1976	Cincinnati (NL)	New York (AL)	4-0
1977	New York (AL)	Los Angeles (NL)	4-2
1978	New York (AL)	Los Angeles (NL)	4-2
1979	Pittsburgh (NL)	Baltimore (AL)	4-3
1980	Philadelphia (NL)	Kansas City (AL)	4-2

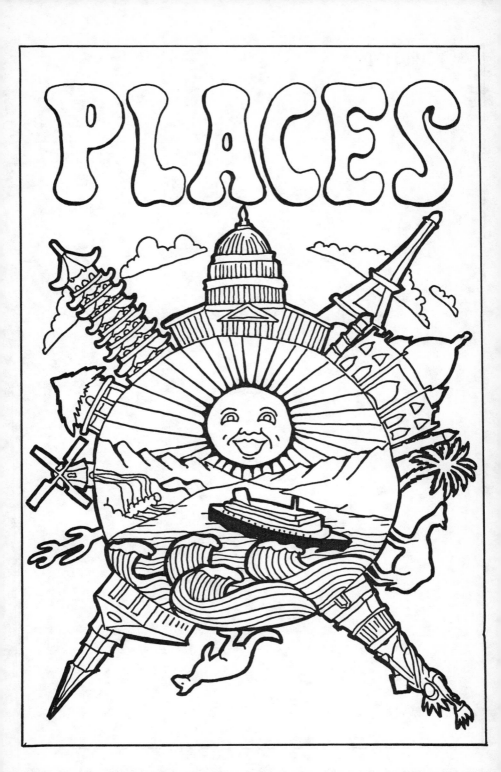

YOUR LIST

FAMOUS ℬATTLE SITES

Site	Date	Location	War
Troy	1193 B.C.	Asia Minor	Trojan War
Marathon	490 B.C.	Greece	Greeks Vs. Persians
Syracuse	413 B.C.	Sicily	Peleponnesian War
Issus	333 B.C.	Syria	Alexander's Macedonian Conquest
Arbela	331 B.C.	Mesopotamia	Alexander's Macedonian Conquest
Rome	410	Italy	Wars of the Western Empire
Tours	732	France	Moslem Invasion
Hastings	1066	Britian	Norman Conquest
Orleans	1429	France	Hundred Years War
Bunker Hill	1775	Massachusetts	US Revolutionary War
Lexington & Concord	1775	Massachusetts	US Revolutionary War
Yorktown	1781	Virginia	US Revolutionary War
New Orleans	1815	Louisiana	War of 1812
Waterloo	1815	Belgium	Napoleon's 100 Days
Alamo	1836	Texas	Mexican War
Vicksburg	1863	Mississippi	Civil War
Gettysburg	1863	Pennsylvania	Civil War
Appamattox	1865	Virginia	Civil War
Little Big Horn	1876	Montana	Sioux Indian Wars
Verdun	1916	France	WWI
Argonne Forest	1918	France	WWI
Battle of Britian	1940	Britian	WWII
Tobruk	1941	Libya	WWII
Bataan	1942	Philippines	WWII
Coral Sea	1942	Australia	WWII
Midway	1942	Midway Island	WWII
Guadalcanal	1943	Solomon Islands	WWII
Salerno	1943	Italy	WWII
Normandy	1944	France	WWII
Battle of the Bulge	1944	Belgium	WWII

TEN LARGEST CITIES (METROPOLITAN AREAS) OF THE WORLD

	City	Population
1.	New York City, NY	16,962,000 (est. 1977)
2.	Mexico City, Mexico	13,993,866 (est. 1978)
3.	Tokyo, Japan	11,695,150 (est. 1977)
4.	Los Angeles-Long Beach, CA	10,605,000 (est. 1977)
5.	Shanghai, China	10,000,000 (est. 1978)
6.	Buenos Aires, Argentina	9,749,000 (est. 1978)
7.	Paris, France	8,547,625 (census, 1975)
8.	Peking, China	8,000,000 (est. 1978)
9.	Moscow, USSR	7,909,000 (est. 1978)
10.	Chicago, Illinois	7,662,000 (est. 1977)

CONTINENTS

Name	Approximate Area in Square Miles
Asia	16,000,000
Africa	11,500,000
North America	9,385,000
South America	6,850,000
Antarctica	5,000,000
Europe	3,700,000
Australia	2,948,360

COUNTRIES OF THE WORLD

Country	Capital
AFRICA	
Algeria	Algiers
Angola	Luanda
Benin	Porto-Novo, Cotonou
Botswana	Gaborone
Burundi	Bujumbura
Cameroon	Yaounde
Central African Republic	Bangui
Chad	N'Djamena
Comoros	Moroni
Congo	Brazzaville
Djibouti	Djibouti
Egypt	Cairo
Equatorial Guinea	Malabo

(cont.)

Country	Capital
Ethiopia	Addis Ababa
Gabon	Libreville
Gambia	Banjul
Ghana	Accra
Guinea	Conakry
Guinea-Bissau	Bissau
Ivory Coast	Abidjan
Kenya	Nairobi
Lesotho	Maseru
Liberia	Monrovia
Libya	Tripoli
Madagascar	Tananarive
Malawi	Lilongwe
Mali	Bamako
Mauritania	Nouakchott
Mauritius	Port Louis
Morocco	Rabat
Mozambique	Maputo
Niger	Niamey
Nigeria	Lagos
Rwanda	Kigali
Senegal	Dakar
Sierra Leone	Freetown
Somalia	Mogadishu
Republic of South Africa	Cape Town (legislative)
	Pretoria (administrative)
	Bloemfontein (judicial)
Sudan	Khartoum
Swaziland	Mbabane
Tanzania	Dar-es-Salaam
Togo	Lomé
Tunisia	Tunis
Uganda	Kampala
Upper Volta	Ouagadougou
Zaire	Kinshasa
Zambia	Lusaka
Zimbabwe	Salisbury

ASIA

Country	Capital
Afghanistan	Kabul
Bangladesh	Dacca

(cont.)

Country	ASIA (cont.)	Capital
Bhutan		Thimphu
Burma		Rangoon
Cambodia		Phnom Penh
China		Peking
China (Taiwan)		Taipei
Cyprus		Nicosia
India		New Delhi
Indonesia		Jakarta
Iran		Teheran
Iraq		Baghdad
Israel		Jerusalem
Jordan		Amman
Kiribati		Tarawa
North Korea		Pyongyang
South Korea		Seoul
Kuwait		Kuwait
Laos		Vientiane
Lebanon		Beirut
Malaysia		Kuala Lampur
Maldives		Male
Mongolia		Ulan Bator
Nauru		Yaren
Nepal		Kathmandu
Oman		Muscat
Pakistan		Islamabad
Papua New Guinea		Port Moresby
Philippines		Quezon City (Manila is defacto capital)
Qatar		Doha
Samoa		Apia
Saudi Arabia		Riyadh
Singapore		Singapore
Solomon Islands		Honiara
Sri Lanka		Colombo
Syria		Damascus
Thailand		Bangkok
Turkey		Ankara
Union of Soviet Socialist Republics		Moscow
United Arab Emirates		Abu Dhabi
Vietnam		Hanoi
Yemen		Sana
South Yemen		Aden
Bahrain		Manama

Country	Capital

<u>AUSTRALIA</u>

Australia	Canberra

<u>EUROPE</u>

Country	Capital
Albania	Tirana
Andorra	Andorra la Vella
Austria	Vienna
Belgium	Brussels
Bulgaria	Sofia
Czechoslovakia	Prague
Denmark	Copenhagen
Finland	Helsinki
France	Paris
Germany (East)	East Berlin
Germany (West)	Bonn
Greece	Athens
Hungary	Budapest
Iceland	Reykjavik
Ireland	Dublin
Italy	Rome
Liechtenstein	Vaduz
Luxembourg	Luxembourg
Monaco	Monaco
Netherlands	Amsterdam
Norway	Oslo
Poland	Warsaw
Portugal	Lisbon
Romania	Bucharest
San Marino	San Marino
Spain	Madrid
Sweden	Stockholm
Switzerland	Bern
United Kingdom of Great Britain and Northern Ireland	London
Vatican City	Vatican
Yugoslavia	Belgrade
Malta	Valletta

(cont.)

Country	*Capital*

ISLAND COUNTRIES

Fiji	Suva
New Zealand	Wellington
Seychelles	Victoria
Tonga	Nuku'alofa

NORTH AMERICA

United States	Washington, D.C.
Bahamas	Nassau
Barbados	Bridgetown
Canada	Ottawa
Costa Rica	San Jose
Cuba	Havana
Dominica	Roseau
Dominican Republic	Santa Domingo
El Salvador	San Salvador
Guatemala	Guatemala City
Haiti	Port-au-Prince
Jamaica	Kingston
Mexico	Mexico City
Nicaragua	Managua
Panama	Panama
Saint Lucia	Castries
Saint Vincent & Grenadines	Kingstown
Grenada	Saint George's
Honduras	Tegucigalpa
Trinidad & Tobago	Port-of-Spain

SOUTH AMERICA

Argentina	Buenos Aires
Bolivia	Sucre, La Paz
Brazil	Brasilia
Chile	Santiago
Colombia	Bogota
Ecuador	Quito
Guyana	Georgetown
Paraguay	Asuncion
Peru	Lima
Suriname	Paramaribo
Uruguay	Montevideo
Venezuela	Caracas

TWELVE LARGEST COUNTRIES IN THE WORLD

Country	Approximate Population
1. China	893,873,000
2. India	662,958,000
3. Russia	269,306,000
4. United States	222,502,000
5. Indonesia	154,340,000
6. Brazil	126,497,000
7. Japan	118,747,000
8. Bangladesh	92,181,000
9. Pakistan	81,451,000
10. Nigeria	72,031,000
11. Mexico	71,524,000
12. West Germany	61,991,000

MAJOR DESERTS OF THE WORLD

Arabian (Saudi Arabia)
Atacama (western South America)
Black Rock Desert (Nevada, US)
DashtiKavir or Great Salt Desert (north central Iran)
Gibson (Australia)
Gobi (Mongolia)
Great Indian (northeastern India)
Great Salt Lake (Utah, US)
Great Sandy (northwestern Australia)
Great Victoria (southwestern Australia)
Kalihari (southern Africa)
Kara Kum (U.S.S.R, Asia)
Kyzyl Kum (U.S.S.R., central Asia)
Mojave (southwestern US)
Namib (southwestern Africa)
Painted (southwestern US)
Rub' al Khali, also called Arabian or Empty Quarter (Saudi Arabia)
Sahara Desert Region (northern Africa) includes:
     Eastern Desert
     Libyan Desert
     Nubian Desert
     Western Desert
Sonoran (southwestern US and northwestern Mexico)
Syrian (Arabia, Syria, Iraq, Transjordan)
Takla Makan (western China)

OCEANS OF THE WORLD

Name	Area in Square Miles
Pacific	70,000,000
Atlantic	31,830,000
Indian	28,350,000
Arctic	5,440,000

MAJOR RIVERS OF THE WORLD

AFRICA:
Congo (Zaire, Congo) - 2,900 mi.
Niger (Guinea, Mali, Niger, Nigeria) - 2,600 mi.
Nile (Egypt, Sudan, Uganda) - 4,149 mi.
Orange (South Africa) - 1,350 mi.
Zambezi (Zambia, Zimbabwe/Rhodesia) - 1,600 mi.

ASIA / MIDDLE EAST:
Amur (western Asia) - 2,704 mi.
Brahmaputra (Tibet, India) - 1,680 mi.
Euphrates (Iraq, Syria, Turkey) - 2,235 mi.
Indus (Pakistan) - 1,700 mi.
Irrawaddy (Burma) - 1,325 mi.
Lena (U.S.S.R.) - 2,648 mi.
Mekong (southeastern Asia) - 2,600 mi.
Salween (southeastern Asia) - 1,750 mi.
Sungari (southeastern Manchuria) - 800 mi.
Tigris (Iraq, Turkey) - 1,150 mi.

AUSTRALIA:
Darling - 1,160 mi.
Murray - 1,200 mi.

CANADA:
Churchill - 1,000 mi.
Fraser - 850 mi.
Mackenzie - 2,635 mi.
Peace - 1,065 mi.
Saint Lawrence - 1,900 mi.
Saskatchewan - 1,205 mi.
Yukon (also in Alaska) - 1,979 mi.

CHINA:
Si - 1,000 mi.
Yangtze - 3,400 mi.
Yellow (also known as Hwang) - 2,700 mi.

EUROPE:
Danube (Germany, Austria, Hungary, Yugoslavia, Romania) - 1,725 mi.
Rhine (Germany, Netherlands) - 820 mi.
Tisza (Hungary, Yugoslavia) - 800 mi.

(cont.)

INDIA:
Brahmaputra - 1,680 mi.
Ganges - 1,650 mi.

SOUTH AMERICA:
Amazon (Brazil, Peru) - 3,900 mi.
Japurá (northwestern) - 1,750 mi.
Madeira (Brazil) - 2,000 mi.
Magdalena (Columbia) - 1,000 mi.
Orinoco (Venezuela) - 1,600 mi.
Paraná (southeast central) - 2,450 mi.
Paraguay (south central) - 1,500 mi.
Pilcomayo (south central) - 1,000 mi.
Purus (Peru, Brazil) - 2,000 mi.
Rio Negro (Columbia, Venezuela, Brazil) - 1,400 mi.
Saõ Francisco (Brazil) - 1,800 mi.
Tocantins (Brazil) - 1,700 mi.
Uruguay (southeastern) - 1,000 mi.

U.S.:
Arkansas - 1,450 mi.
Brazos - 870 mi.
Canadian - 906 mi.
Colorado (also in Mexico) - 1,450 mi.
Columbia (also in Canada) - 1,214 mi.
Mississippi - 3,870 mi.
Missouri - 2,720 mi.
Ohio - 980 mi.
Platte-North Platte - 990 mi.
Red - 1,018 mi.
Rio Grande (also in Mexico) - 1,885 mi.
Snake - 1,038 mi.
Tennessee - 862 mi.

U.S.S.R.:
Amu-Darya - 1,550 mi.
Angara (also in Asia) - 1,100 mi.
Don - 1,222 mi.
Dnieper - 1,418 mi.
Dniester - 852 mi.
Kama - 1,200 mi.
Kolyma - 1,110 mi.
Lena (also in Asia) - 2,648 mi.
Ob-Irtysh - 3,200 mi.
Olenek (also in Asia) - 1,325 mi.
Pechora - 1,125 mi.
Syr-Darya - 1,680 mi.
Ural - 1,574 mi.
Volga - 2,290 mi.
Yenisey - 2,364 mi.

MAJOR SEAS OF THE WORLD

Name	Location
Adriatic	an arm of the Mediterranean, southeast of Italy
Aegean	between Asia Minor and Greece
Arafura	between New Guinea and Australia
Baltic	an arm of the Atlantic Ocean in northern Europe
Barents	an area of the Arctic Ocean, north of Norway and the USSR
Beaufort	part of the Arctic Ocean, north of Alaska and Canada
Bering	an area of the northern Pacific Ocean between Alaska and Siberia
Bismark	in the western Pacific Ocean
Black	between Europe and Asia
Caribbean	an arm of the Atlantic Ocean between North America and South America
Caspian	between Europe and Asia — the world's largest inland body of water
China	part of the Pacific Ocean between Japan and the Malay Peninsula; divided into the East China Sea and the South China Sea
Coral	area of the Pacific Ocean between Australia and New Hebrides
Dead	lake between Israel and Jordan
Hudson Bay	an inland sea in the Northwest Territory, Canada
Mediterranean	an inland sea bordered by Europe, Africa and Asia
North	an arm of the Atlantic Ocean between northern Europe and Great Britian
Red	an inland sea between Arabia and Africa
Sea of Japan	west of Japan
Sea of Okhotsk	in the eastern USSR and Asia

SITES OF OLYMPIC GAMES

Summer	Year	Winter
Athens	1896	—
Paris	1900	—
St. Louis	1904	—
London	1908	—
Stockholm	1912	—
Antwerp	1920	—
Paris	1924	Chamonix
Amsterdam	1928	St. Moritz
Los Angeles	1932	Lake Placid
Berlin	1936	Garmish-Partenkirchen

(cont.)

Summer	Year	Winter
London	1948	St. Moritz
Helsinki	1952	Oslo
Melbourne	1956	Cortina
Rome	1960	Squaw Valley
Tokyo	1964	Innsbruck
Mexico City	1968	Grenoble
Munich	1972	Sapporo
Montreal	1976	Innsbruck
Moscow	1980	Lake Placid

U.S. INFORMATION

U.S. STATES AND CAPITALS

State	Admitted to Union	Capital	ZIP Abbreviation
Delaware	1787	Dover	DE
New Jersey	1787	Trenton	NJ
Pennsylvania	1787	Harrisburg	PA
Connecticut	1788	Hartford	CT
Georgia	1788	Atlanta	GA
Maryland	1788	Annapolis	MD
Massachusetts	1788	Boston	MA
New Hampshire	1788	Concord	NH
New York	1788	Albany	NY
South Carolina	1788	Columbia	SC
Virginia	1788	Richmond	VA
North Carolina	1789	Raleigh	NC
Rhode Island	1790	Providence	RI

(13 Original States — Ratified the US Constitution)

State	Admitted to Union	Capital	ZIP Abbreviation
Vermont	1791	Montpelier	VT
Kentucky	1792	Frankfort	KY
Tennessee	1796	Nashville	TN
Ohio	1803	Columbus	OH
Louisiana	1812	Baton Rouge	LA
Indiana	1816	Indianapolis	IN
Mississippi	1817	Jackson	MS
Illinois	1818	Springfield	IL

(cont.)

U.S. STATES AND CAPITALS (cont.)

State	Admitted to Union	Capital	ZIP Abbreviation
Alabama	1819	Montgomery	AL
Maine	1820	Augusta	ME
Missouri	1821	Jefferson City	MO
Arkansas	1836	Little Rock	AR
Michigan	1837	Lansing	MI
Florida	1845	Tallahassee	FL
Texas	1845	Austin	TX
Iowa	1846	Des Moines	IA
Wisconsin	1848	Madison	WI
California	1850	Sacramento	CA
Minnesota	1858	St. Paul	MN
Oregon	1859	Salem	OR
Kansas	1861	Topeka	KS
West Virginia	1863	Charleston	WV
Nevada	1864	Carson City	NV
Nebraska	1867	Lincoln	NE
Colorado	1876	Denver	CO
North Dakota	1889	Bismarck	ND
South Dakota	1889	Pierre	SD
Montana	1889	Helena	MT
Washington	1889	Olympia	WA
Idaho	1890	Boise	ID
Wyoming	1890	Cheyenne	WY
Utah	1896	Salt Lake City	UT
Oklahoma	1907	Oklahoma City	OK
New Mexico	1912	Santa Fe	NM
Arizona	1912	Phoenix	AZ
Alaska	1958	Juneau	AK
Hawaii	1959	Honolulu	HI

OUTLYING US AREAS

Name	Status	Capital	ZIP Abbreviation
American Samoa	US Territory	Pago Pago	—
Guam (Mariana Islands)	US Territory	Agana	GU
Howland, Baker & Jarvis Islands	US Possessions	uninhabited	—
Johnston Atoll	US Possession		—
Kingman Reef	US Possession	uninhabited	—
Midway Island	US Possession		—
Navassa Island	US Possession	uninhabited	—
Palmyra Island (atoll)	US Possession	uninhabited	—
Puerto Rico	Commonwealth	San Juan	PR
Trust Territory of the Pacific (Carolines, Marshalls and Marianas; also called Micronesia)	Trust Territory		—
Virgin Islands	US Territory	Charlotte Amalie	VI
Wake Island	US Possession		—

TEN LARGEST CITIES IN THE U.S.

Rank	City	Estimated Population (1977)
1	New York, New York	7,298,000
2	Chicago, Illinois	3,063,000
3	Los Angeles, California	2,761,000
4	Philadelphia, Pennsylvania	1,778,000
5	Houston, Texas	1,555,000
6	Detroit, Michigan	1,290,000
7	Dallas, Texas	845,000
8	Baltimore, Maryland	804,000
9	San Diego, California	800,000
10	San Antonio, Texas	793,000

(cont.)

NATIONAL PARKS & MONUMENTS

ALABAMA
Russell Cave (NM)

ALASKA
Aniakchak (NM)
Bering Land Bridge (NM)
Cape Krusenstern (NM)
Denali (NM)
Gates of the Arctic (NM)
Glacier Bay (NM)
Katmai (NM)
Kenai Fiords (NM)
Klondike Gold Rush (NHP)
Kobuk Valley (NM)
Lake Clark (NM)
Mount McKinley (NP)
Noatak (NM)
Sitka (NHP)
Wrangell-St. Elias (NM)
Yukon-Charley (NM)

ARIZONA
Canyon de Chelly (NM)
Casa Grande Ruins (NM)
Chiricahua (NM)
Grand Canyon (NP)
Hohokam Pima (NM)
Montezuma Castle (NM)
Navajo (NM)
Organ Pipe Cactus (NM)
Petrified Forest (NP)
Pipe Spring (NM)
Saguaro (NM)
Sunset Crater (NM)
Tonto (NM)
Tumacacori (NM)
Tuzigoot (NM)
Walnut Canyon (NM)
Wupatki (NM)

ARKANSAS
Hot Springs   (NP)

CALIFORNIA
Cabrillo   (NM)
Channel Islands   (NM)
Death Valley   (NM)
Devils Postpile   (NM)
Joshua Tree   (NM)
Kings Canyon   (NP)
Lassen Volcanic   (NP)
Lava Beds   (NM)
Muir Woods   (NM)
Pinnacles   (NM)
Redwood   (NP)
Sequoia   (NP)
Yosemite   (NP)

COLORADO
Black Canyon of the Gunnison   (NM)
Colorado   (NM)
Dinosaur   (NM)
Florissant Fossil Beds   (NM)
Great Sand Dunes   (NM)
Hovenweep   (NM)
Mesa Verde   (NP)
Rocky Mountain   (NP)
Yucca House   (NM)

FLORIDA
Biscayne   (NM)
Castillo de San Marcos   (NM)
Everglades   (NP)
Fort Jefferson   (NM)
Fort Matanzas   (NM)

GEORGIA
Fort Frederica   (NM)
Fort Pulaski   (NM)
Ocmulgee   (NM)

GUAM
War in the Pacific   (NHP)

(cont.)

NATIONAL PARKS & MONUMENTS (cont.)

HAWAII
Haleakala   (NP)
Hawaii Volcanoes   (NP)
Kaloko-Honokohau   (NHP)
Puuhonua o Honaunau   (NHP)

IDAHO
Craters of the Moon   (NM)
Nez Perce   (NHP)

INDIANA
George Rogers Clark   (NHP)

IOWA
Effigy Mounds   (NM)

KENTUCKY
Cumberland Gap   (NHP)
Mammoth Cave   (NP)

MAINE
Acadia   (NP)
St. Croix Island   (NM)

MARYLAND
Chesapeake and Ohio Canal   (NHP)
Fort McHenry   (NM) and Historic Shrine

MASSACHUSETTS
Boston   (NHP)
Lowell   (NHP)
Minute Man   (NHP)

MICHIGAN
Isle Royale   (NP)

MINNESOTA
Grand Portage   (NM)
Pipestone   (NM)
Voyageurs   (NP)

MISSOURI
George Washington Carver (NM)

MONTANA
Custer Battlefield (NM)
Glacier (NP)

NEBRASKA
Agate Fossil Beds (NM)
Homestead (NM)
Scotts Bluff (NM)

NEVADA
Lehman Caves (NM)

NEW JERSEY
Morristown (NHP)

NEW MEXICO
Aztec Ruins (NM)
Bandelier (NM)
Capulin Mountain (NM)
Carlsbad Caverns (NP)
Chaco Canyon (NM)
El Morro (NM)
Fort Union (NM)
Gila Cliff Dwellings (NM)
Gran Quivira (NM)
Pecos (NM)
White Sands (NM)

NEW YORK
Castle Clinton (NM)
Fort Stanwix (NM)
Saratoga (NHP)
Statue of Liberty (NM)

NORTH DAKOTA
Theodore Roosevelt (NP)

OHIO
Mound City Group (NM)

(cont.)

NATIONAL PARKS & MONUMENTS (cont.)

OREGON
Crater Lake   (NP)
John Day Fossil Beds   (NM)
Oregon Caves   (NM)

PENNSYLVANIA
Independence   (NHP)
Valley Forge   (NHP)

PUERTO RICO
AND VIRGIN ISLANDS
Buck Island Reef   (NM)
Virgin Islands   (NP)

SOUTH CAROLINA
Congaree Swamp   (NM)
Fort Sumter   (NM)

SOUTH DAKOTA
Badlands   (NP)
Jewel Cave   (NM)
Wind Cave   (NP)

TENNESSEE
Great Smoky Mountains   (NP)

TEXAS
Alibates Flint Quarries   (NM)
Big Bend   (NP)
Guadalupe Mountains   (NP)

UTAH
Arches   (NP)
Bryce Canyon   (NP)
Canyonlands   (NP)
Capitol Reef   (NP)
Cedar Breaks   (NM)
Natural Bridges   (NM)
Rainbow Bridge   (NM)
Timpanogos Cave   (NM)
Zion   (NP)

VIRGINIA
Appomattox Court House   (NHP)
Booker T. Washington (NM)
Colonial (NHP)
George Washington Birthplace (NM)
Shenandoah (NP)

WASHINGTON
Klondike Gold Rush   (NHP)
Mount Rainier   (NP)
North Cascades   (NP)
Olympic   (NP)
San Juan Island   (NHP)

WEST VIRGINIA
Harpers Ferry   (NHP)

WYOMING
Devils Tower   (NM)
Fossil Butte   (NM)
Grand Teton   (NP)
Yellowstone   (NP)

NP — National Park
NM — National Monument
NHP — National Historic Park

AUSTRALIAN STATES AND THEIR CAPITALS

States	*Capitals*
Australian Capital Territory (not a state)	Canberra
New South Wales	Sydney
Queensland	Brisbane
Victoria	Melbourne
Tasmania	Hobart
South Australia	Adelaide
Western Australia	Perth
Northern Territory	Darwin

CANADIAN PROVINCES AND THEIR CAPITALS

Provinces	*Capitals*
Alberta	Edmonton
British Columbia	Victoria
Manitoba	Winnipeg
New Brunswick	Fredericton
Newfoundland	St. John's
Nova Scotia	Halifax
Ontario	Toronto
Prince Edward Island	Charlottetown
Quebec	Quebec City
Saskatchewan	Regina

MEXICAN STATES AND TERRITORIES

States and Territories	Capital
1. Aguascalientes	Aguascalientes
2. Baja California	Mexicali
3. Baja California Sur (territory)	—
4. Campeche	Campeche
5. Chiapas	Tuxtla Gutierrez
6. Chihuahua	Chihuahua
7. Coahuila	Saltillo
8. Colima	Colima
9. Distrito Federal	México City
10. Durango	Durango
11. Guanajuato	Leon
12. Guerrero	Chilpancingo
13. Hidalgo	Lulancingo
14. Jalisco	Guadalajára
15. México	Toluca
16. Michoacán	Morelia
17. Morelos	Cuernavaca
18. Nayarit	Tepic
19. Nuevo Léon	Guadalupe
20. Oaxaca	Oaxaca
21. Puebla	Puebla
22. Querétaro	Querétaro
23. Quintana Roo (territory)	—
24. San Luis Potosí	San Luis Potosí
25. Sinaloa	Culiacán
26. Sonora	Hermosillo
27. Tabasco	Villahermosa
28. Tamaulipas	Ciudad Victoria
29. Tlaxcla	Tlaxcla
30. Veracruz	Jalapa Enríquez
31. Yucatán	Mérida
32. Zacatecas	Zacatecas

THINGS

YOUR LIST

BRAILLE ALPHABET

LINE 1

a b c d e f g h i j
1 2 3 4 5 6 7 8 9 0

Line 1, consisting of the first 10 letters of the alphabet is formed with dots 1,2,4,5 in the upper part of the braille cell. When preceded by the numeric indicator these cells have number values.

LINE 2

k l m n o p q r s t

Line 2 adds dot 3 to each of the characters of Line 1.

LINE 3

u v x y z and for of the with

Line 3 adds dots 3 and 6 to each of the characters of the first line.

LINE 4

ch gh sh th wh ed er ou ow w

Line 4 adds dot 6 to each of the characters of the first line.

LINE 5

, ; : . en ! () "/? in "

Line 5 repeats the characters of Line 1 in the lower portion of the cell, using dots 2,3,5,6. Most of the characters have punctuation values.

LINE 6

st ing # ar ' —

Line 6 is formed with dots 3,4,5,6.

```
1 •   • 4
2 •   • 5
3 •   • 6
```

LINE 7

general accent sign | used for two-celled contractions | italic sign; decimal point | letter sign | capital sign

Line 7 is formed with dots 4,5,6.

Although punctuation and letter values are given for each configuration, most of the configurations have other meanings when used in conjunction with different braille characters.

(cont.)

ALPHABET FOR THE DEAF

GREEK ALPHABET

A α	Alpha		N ν	Nu
B β	Beta		Ξ ξ	Xi
Γ γ	Gamma		O o	Omicron
Δ δ	Delta		Π π	Pi
E ε	Epsilon		P ρ	Rhō
Z ζ	Zēta		Σ σ ς	Sigma
H η	Ēta		T τ	Tau
Θ θ	Thēta		Υ υ	Upsilon
I ι	Iota		Φ φ	Phi
K κ	Kappa		X χ	Khi
Λ λ	Lambda		Ψ ψ	Psi
M μ	Mu		Ω ω	Ōmega

MORSE CODE

A	..	J	.----	S	...	2	..---	
B	....	K	..-	T	-	3	...--	
C	..-.	L	..-.	U	..-	4	....-	
D	...	M	--	V	....	5	.....	
E	.	N	..	W	.--	6	-....	
F	..-.	O	---	X	-..-	7	--...	
G	--.	P	.--.	Y	-.--	8	---..	
H	....	Q	--.-	Z	--..	9	----.	
I	..	R	.-.	1	.----	0	-----	

ANIMAL FAMILY NAMES

Female	Male	Offspring
goose	gander	gosling
cow, heifer	bull	calf
duck	drake	duckling
ewe	ram	lamb
sow	hog	piglet
mare	stallion	colt (male)
		filly (female)
bitch	dog	pup (puppy)
hen	rooster	chick
nanny	goat	kid
doe	buck	fawn
vixen	fox	cub
tigress	tiger	cub
lioness	lion	cub
she-bear	bear	cub

COLLECTIVE NOUNS FOR ANIMALS

a bevy of larks or quail
a brood of young birds
a colony of ants
a covey of partridges
a drift of swine or hogs
a drove of sheep
a fall of woodcocks
a flight of birds (in flight together)
a flock of sheep or goats (herded by humans)
a gaggle of geese
a gam of whales
a gang of buffalo or elk
a herd of cattle
a hive of bees
a horde of animals (a throng)
a kennel of dogs (all under one roof)
a kindle of kittens (also a litter of same)
a pack of wolves or grouse
a pride of lions
a school of fish

(cont.)

a shoal of whales
a cast of falcons or hawks (cast off at the same time)
a cete of badgers
a covert of coots
a litter (total number of offsprings produced at one birth)
a muster or flock of peacocks
a pod (small herd) of seals
a rout of wolves (company in movement)
a shrewdness (or company) of apes
a skein (or flight) of wild fowl
a skulk (congregation) of foxes
a sloth of bears
a sounder (herd) of wild hogs
a spring (flock) of teal
a stable of horses (all under one roof)
a swarm of insects (group in flight or movement)
a watch (flock) of nightingales
a wisp (or flock) of snipe

BIRTHSTONES AND FLOWERS

	BIRTHSTONES		FLOWERS
Month	*Old*	*New*	
January	Garnet	Garnet	Carnation
February	Amethyst	Amethyst	Violet
March	Jasper	Bloodstone or Aquamarine	Jonquil
April	Sapphire	Diamond	Sweet Pea
May	Agate	Emerald	Lily of the Valley
June	Emerald	Pearl or Moonstone	Rose
July	Onyx	Ruby	Larkspur
August	Carnelian	Peridot or Sardonyx	Gladiola
September	Chrysolite	Sapphire	Aster
October	Aquamarine	Tourmaline or Opal	Calendula
November	Topaz	Topaz	Crysanthemum
December	Ruby	Turquoise or Lapis Lazuli	Narcissus

CALENDAR INFORMATION

History

The calendar which is now in use in many parts of the world is called the Gregorian Calendar. It was introduced by Pope Gregory XIII in 1582, and was adopted by England and America in 1752. This calendar replaced the Julian calendar which Julius Caesar introduced in 46 B.C. Before that, the ancient Romans used a lunar calendar (one based on the moon).

The word ''calendar'' comes from the Latin ''kalendarium'' which means a ''moneylender's account book.'' That word comes from the Latin ''kalendae'' which was the first day of each month, and the day of the new moon. Interest owed to moneylenders was due on the ''calend'' or the first day of each month; hence the connection.

Days of the Week

Sunday — from Old English ''sunnandæg'' — day of the sun
Monday — from Old English ''mōnan dæg'' — day of the moon
Tuesday — from Old English ''tīwesdæg'' — day of Tiu, the god of war and the sky
Wednesday — from Old English ''Wōdenesdæg'' — day of Woden, the Teutonic god identified with Odin, the supreme diety in Norse mythology
Thursday — from Old English ''thūr(e)s dæg'' — influenced by the Old Norse ''thorsdagr'' which means ''day of Thor,'' the god of thunder in Norse mythology
Friday — from Old English ''frīgedæg'' — day of Frigg, the wife of Odin and goddess of love in Norse mythology
Saturday — from Old English ''sæternesdæg'' — Saturn's day (the Roman god identified with the Greek Titan who ruled the universe until overthrown by his son Zeus, according to Greek mythology)

Months of the Year

January — from the Latin month of Janus, the festival month of the ancient Roman god of gates and doorways who was always shown with two faces looking in opposite directions
February — from the Latin ''februarius'' which was the Latin festival of purification, held the 15th day of that month
March — named after Mars, the Roman god of war
April — named after Aphroditē, the Greek goddess of love and beauty
May — named after Maia, a Roman goddess of spring
June — from the Latin month consecrated to Juno, the Roman goodess of marriage and of the well-being of women
July — named for Julius Caesar
August — named for Augustus Caesar
September — from the Latin ''septem'' meaning ''seven'' because it was once the seventh month of the Roman calendar
October — from the Latin ''octo'' meaning ''eight'' because it was once the eighth month of the Roman calendar
November — from the Latin ''novem'' meaning ''nine'' because it was once the ninth month of the Roman calendar
December — from the Latin ''decem'' meaning ''ten'' because it was once the tenth month of the Roman calendar

SOME CAREER OPTIONS

AGRI-BUSINESS AND NATURAL RESOURCES

Animal Husbandry	Geologist	Rancher
Animal Research	Geophysicist	Rig Builder
Cowboy	Microbiologist	Soil Conservationist
Entomologist	Miner	Soil Scientist
Farmer	Oil Refinery Worker	Veterinarian
Forester	Petroleum Engineer	Wild Life Scientist

BUSINESS AND OFFICE

Accountant	Fiscal Manager	Office Manager
Bookkeeper	General Office Clerk	Office Supervisor
Clerk Typist	Insurance Agent	Real Estate Broker
Computer Programmer	Keypunch Operator	Secretary
Dealership Operator	Machine Transcriber	Systems Analyst

COMMUNICATION AND MEDIA

Darkroom Technician	Journalist	Sign Painter
Display Technician	Layout Person	Telephone Worker
Editor	Photographer	TV and Radio Workers
Electronics Engineer	Reporter	Writer

CONSTRUCTION

Architect	Engineer	Paper Hanger
Bricklayer	Floor Covering Installer	Plasterer
Carpenter	Glazier	Plumber and Pipefitter
Cement Mason	Iron Worker	Roofer
Construction Laborer	Metal Worker	Sheet Metal Worker
Electrician	Painter	Stonemason

CONSUMER AND HOMEMAKING

Chef	Cook	Home Management
Cleaner	Dietician	Counselor
Clothing Designer	Food Service Industry	Housekeeper
Clothing Inspector	Worker	Interior Decorator
Clothing Machine	Furniture Maker	Laundry Worker
Operator	Furniture Refinisher	Product Demonstrator
Consumer Counselor	Home Economist	Upholsterer

ENVIRONMENT

Air Analyst	Hydroponic Plant	Mine and Dump
Bacteriologist	Culturist	Restoration Controller
Conservationist	Landscape Architect	Pollution Control Engineer
Exterminator	Marine Biologist	Sanitation Worker
Game Warden	Meteorologist	Soil Analyst
Gardener		Urban Planner

FINE ARTS AND HUMANITIES

Actor	Dancer	Industrial Designer
Artist Manager	Fashion Designer	Music Composer
Cameraman	Film Production	Painter
Costume Designer	Foreign Language	Printmaker
Costume Maker	Broadcaster	Sculptor
Creative Writer	Illustrator	Stage Manager

(cont.)

HEALTH SERVICES

Biochemist	Inhalation Therapist	Pharmacist
Biophysicist	Licensed Practical Nurse	Physical Therapist
Dental Assistant	Medical Laboratory Worker	Physician
Dental Hygienist	Medical Photographer	Podiatrist
Dentist	Medical Records Librarian	Registered Nurse
Dietician	Optometrist	Veterinarian

HOSPITALITY, RECREATION, AND LEISURE

Bellmen and Bell Captain	Movie Projectionist	Sports Director
Bus Driver	Museum Curator	Tour Guides
Chef	Museum Guard	Travel Agent
Coach	Park Ranger	Waiter/Waitress
Hotel or Motel Manager	Professional Athlete	

MANUFACTURING

Assembly Line Operator	Plant Manager	Product Tester
Distributor	Product Designer	Product Transporter
Industrial Engineer	Product Developer	Retailer
Industrial Psychologist	Product Inspector	Wholesaler

MARINE SCIENCE

Deep Sea Diver	Ocean Fishing Boat	Offshore Mineral Driller
Fish Hatcher and Raiser	Operator	Seafood Inspector
Marine Researcher	Oceanographic Mapper	Underwater Workers

MARKET AND DISTRIBUTION

Store Owner/Manager	Marketing Researcher	Salesman
Management Personnel	Purchasing Agent	Sales Promotion/Publicity

PERSONAL SERVICES

Animal Trainer	Building Custodian	Masseur
Barber	Hair Stylist	Private Household Worker
Bartender	Makeup Technician	Watchman

PUBLIC SERVICE

Agricultural Advisor	Immigration Inspector	Port Authority Workers
Army	Internal Revenue Service	Post Office Worker
Building Inspector	Judge	Public Recorder
Coast Guard	Librarian	Registrar and Licenser of
Counselor—Rehabilitation	Maintenance Worker	Cars
Customs Official	Marine Corps	Research Worker
Elected Official	Navy	Sanitation People
Employment Counselor	Plant and Animal	Teachers
Engineer	Inspectors	Traffic Controller
Fireman	Police Force	

TRANSPORTATION

Aircraft Mechanic	Flight Engineer	Steward and Stewardess
Airline Dispatcher	Locomotive Worker	Taxi Driver
Air Traffic Controller	Merchant Mariner	Track Worker
Automobile Mechanic	Pilot	Traffic Agent
Bus Driver	Signal Worker	Truck Driver
Conductor	Station Agent	Truck Mechanic

Name	Description	Weather Prediction
cumulus	piles of clouds, like towers	fair weather
cumulonimbus	thunderheads (large, dark cumulus)	thunderstorm
stratus	smooth layers of low clouds	maybe slight drizzle or snow
stratocumulus	piles of clouds in layers	maybe slight drizzle or snow
nimbostratus	smooth layers of gray clouds	continuous precipitation
altostratus	a thick sheet of gray or bluish color	rain or snow
altocumulus	piles of clouds in wavy lines	rain or snow
cirrus	feather-like clouds, (made of ice crystals)	fair weather
cirrostratus	thin sheets of clouds; causes halo around sun or moon	rain or snow within 24 hours
cirrocumulus	like cotton balls in wavy lines	fair weather

FIRST AID KIT SUPPLIES

adhesive dressings
adhesive tape
alcohol
antiseptic for minor cuts, etc.
bicarbonate of soda
calamine lotion
candles
cloth to make tourniquet
cotton
eye dropper
flashlight and extra batteries
gauze bandages
hot water bottle
ice bag
ipecac syrup (to induce vomiting)
needles and thread
oral thermometer
petroleum jelly
powdered activated charcoal (to absorb swallowed poisons)
rectal thermometer
safety matches
scissors
sharp knife
single edge razor blades
sterile gauze dressings
sterile saline solution
spirits of ammonia
tweezers

Collect the above and put them in a sturdy box in a dry place. On the outside top of the box, write your doctor's telephone number, the number for your local Poison Control group and the number for your local EMERGENCY Unit.

Check your materials at least once a year to make sure all are in good working order.

JANUARY:
1 — New Year's Day
8 — World Literacy Day
11 — Alice Paul's Birthday
15 — Martin Luther King, Jr.'s Birthday
16 — National Nothing Day
18 — Daniel Webster's Birthday
19 — Robert E. Lee's Birthday
24 — California Gold Discovery Anniversary
27 — Wolfgang Amadeus Mozart's Birthday
Super Bowl
Australia Day
Stephen Foster Week

FEBRUARY:
1 — National Freedom Day
2 — Groundhog Day
4 — Charles Lindbergh's Birthday
8 — Boy Scouts of America Birthday
11 — Thomas Alva Edison's Birthday
12 — Abraham Lincoln's Birthday
14 — League of Women Voters Anniversary
— St. Valentine's Day
22 — George Washington's Birthday
Chinese New Year
National New Idea Week
International Friendship Week
American Music Month
Afro-American History Month

MARCH:
3 — Alexander Graham Bell's Birthday
6 — Elizabeth Barrett Browning's Birthday
— Michelangelo's Birthday
8 — International Working Woman's Day
11 — Johnny Appleseed Day
14 — Albert Einstein's Birthday
17 — St. Patrick's Day
24 — Harry Houdini's Birthday
Vernal Equinox
National Wildlife Week
Return the Borrowed Book Week
National Procrastination Week
Girl Scout Week
National Poison Prevention Week

APRIL:
1 — April Fool's Day
2 — International Children's Book Day
— Hans Christian Andersen's Birthday
3 — Washington Irving's Birthday
7 — World Health Day
13 — Thomas Jefferson's Birthday
18 — Paul Revere's Ride Anniversary
23 — William Shakespeare's Birthday
28 — Arbor Day
Daylight Savings Time Begins
Easter
National Library Week
Bike Safety Week
National Volunteer Week
Earth Week
Canada-US Goodwill Week

MAY:
1 — May Day
4 — Holocaust Day
26 — Al Jolson Day
29 — Patrick Henry's Birthday
— John F. Kennedy's Birthday
31 — Walt Whitman's Birthday
Memorial Day
Armed Forces Day
Mother's Day
Victoria Day (Canada)
National Be Kind to Animals Week
National Music Week
International Pickle Week
Radio Month

JUNE:
3 — Jefferson Davis' Birthday
4 — Teacher's Day
5 — World Environment Day
9 — Queen's Official Birthday (England)
14 — Flag Day
— Harriet Beecher Stowe's Birthday
15 — Magna Carta Day
27 — Helen Keller's Birthday
Father's Day
Summer Solstice
National Humor Week
National Cheeseburger Month

(cont.)

─── HOLIDAYS AND FUN CELEBRATIONS (cont.) ───

JULY:
 1 — Dominion Day (Canada)
   — Birthday of 1st US Postage Stamp
 4 — Independence Day
   — Louis Armstrong's Birthday
 6 — John Paul Jones' Birthday
   — Beatrix Potter's Birthday
12 — Henry David Thoreau's Birthday
15 — Clement Clarke Moore's Birthday
20 — Moon Day
21 — Ernest Hemingway's Birthday
24 — Amelia Earhart's Birthday
30 — Henry Ford's Birthday
National Tom Sawyer Days

AUGUST:
 1 — Canada Civic Holiday
   — Herman Melville's Birthday
 4 — Coast Guard Day
 6 — Hiroshima Day
10 — Herbert Hoover's Birthday
13 — Family Day
   — Berlin Wall Anniversary
15 — Napoleon Bonaparte's Birthday
17 — Davy Crockett's Birthday
19 — Ogden Nash's Birthday
27 — World Frisbee Championship
Woman's Equality Day
National Smile Week
Good Nutrition Month
Sandwich Month

SEPTEMBER:
 5 — First Continental Congress Assembly
     Anniversary
 7 — Queen Elizabeth I's Birthday
13 — Walter Reed's Birthday
17 — Citizenship Day
   — World Peace Day
19 — Mickey Mouse's Anniversary
24 — National Good Neighbor Day
28 — Confucius' Birthday
Autumnal Equinox
Labor Day
American Indian Day
National Rehabilitation Week

OCTOBER:
 1 — Grandparent's Day
 2 — Mahatma Gandhi's Birthday
 4 — Sputnik Day
11 — Eleanor Roosevelt's Birthday
15 — National Poetry Day
16 — Noah Webster's Birthday
22 — Mothers-In-Law Day
24 — United Nations Day
31 — Juliette Low's Birthday
   — Halloween
   — National UNICEF Day
Columbus Day
Apple Tuesday
Thanksgiving Day (Canada)
Return to Standart Time
National Fire Prevention Week
National Employ the Handicapped Week

NOVEMBER:
 4 — Mischief Night (England)
 8 — Dunce Day
11 — Armistice Day
   — Remembrance Day (Canada)
14 — Robert Fulton's Birthday
29 — Louisa May Alcott's Birthday
30 — Samuel Clemen's Birthday
Election Day
Thanksgiving
American Education Week
National Children's Book Week
Latin American Week

DECEMBER:
 7 — Pearl Harbor Day
 8 — James Thurber's Birthday
 9 — Joel Chandler Harris' Birthday
10 — Human Rights Day
12 — National Ding-A-Ling Day
15 — Bill of Rights Day
16 — Ludwig van Beethoven's Birthday
   — Boston Tea Party Anniversary
17 — Wright Brothers Day
20 — Louisiana Purchase Day
25 — Christmas Day
26 — Boxing Day (Canada)
30 — Rudyard Kipling's Birthday
31 — New Year's Eve
Winter Solstice
Underdog Day
French Conversation Week
National Mimicry Week

Instruments of an Orchestra

The String Section:

violin
viola
cello
string base

Woodwind Section:

flute
oboe
clarinet
bassoon
piccolo
English horn

Brass Section:

trumpet
French horn
trombone
tuba

Percussion Section:

timpani (kettle drum)
bells
cymbals
bass drum
gong
snare drum
triangle
xylophone

Other (as called for in score):

harp
harpsichord
organ
piano
saxophone

Basic Denomination	Sub-Denomination	Countries
Afghani	100 puls	Afghanistan
Baht	100 satangs	Thailand
Balboa	100 centesimos	Panama
Bolivar	100 centimos	Venezuela
Cedi	100 pesewa	Ghana
Colon	100 centavos	El Salvador
Colon	100 centimos	Costa Rica
Cordoba	100 centavos	Nicaragua
Cruzeiro	100 centavos	Brazil
Dalasi	100 butut	Gambia
Deutsche mark	100 pfennigs	West Germany
Dinar	100 centimes	Algeria
Dinar	10 dirhams	Kuwait
Dinar	1000 dirhams	Libya
Dinar	1000 fils	Iraq, Jordan, Yemen Democratic People's Republic
Dinar	1000 milliemes	Tunisia
Dinar	100 paras	Yugoslavia
Dirham	100 francs	Morocco
Dollar	100 cents	Australia, Barbados, Canada, Ethiopia, Guyana, Hong Kong, Jamaica, Liberia, Malaysia, New Zealand, Rhodesia, Singapore, Trinidad, Tobago, USA
Dong	100 xu	North Vietnam
Drachma	100 lepta	Greece

Basic Denomination	Sub-Denomination	Countries
Escudo	100 centesimos	Chile
Escudo	100 centavos	Portugal
Forint	100 fillér	Hungary
Franc	100 centimes	Belgium, Burundi, Cameroun, Central African Republic, Chad, Congo (Brazzaville), Dahomey, France, Gabon, Guinea, Ivory Coast, Luxembourg, Malagasy Republic, Mali, Mauritania, Niger, Rwanda, Senegal, Switzerland, Togo, Upper Volta
Gourde	100 centimes	Haiti
Guarani	100 centimos	Paraguay
Guilder	100 cents	Netherlands, Netherlands Antilles, Surinam
Kip	100 at	Laos
Koruna	100 halers	Czechoslovakia
Krona	100 aurar	Iceland
Krona	100 öre	Sweden
Krone	100 öre	Denmark, Norway
Kwacha	100 ngwee	Zambia
Kwacha	100 tambala	Republic of Malawi
Kyat	100 pyas	Burma
Lek	100 quintars	Albania
Lempira	100 centavos	Honduras
Leone	100 cents	Sierra Leone
Leu	100 bani	Rumania
Lev	100 stotinki	Bulgaria

(cont.)

Basic Denomination	Sub-Denomination	Countries
Lira	100 centesimi	Italy
Lira	100 kurus	Turkey
Markka	100 pennis	Finland
Niara	100 kobes	Nigeria
Ostmark	100 pfennigs	East Germany
Peseta	100 centimos	Spain
Peso	100 centavos	Argentina, Bolivia, Columbia, Cuba, Dominican Republic, Mexico, Republic of the Philippines
Peso	100 centesimos	Uraguay
Piaster	100 cents	South Vietnam
Pound	100 agorot	Israel
Pound	100 cents	Malta
Pound	1000 mils	Cyprus
Pound	100 pence	Republic of Ireland, United Kingdom of Great Britain and Northern Ireland
Pound	100 piasters	Egypt, Lebanon, Sudan, Syria
Quetzal	100 centavos	Guatemala
Rand	100 cents	Republic of South Africa
Rial	100 dinars	Iran
Riyal	1000 baiza	Oman
Riyal	40 bugshas	Yemen
Riyal	100 dirhams	Qatar
Riyal	20 qurush	Saudi Arabia

Basic Denomination	Sub-Denomination	Countries
Rupee	100 cents	Ceylon, Mauritius
Rupee	100 larees	Maldive Islands
Rupee	100 paise	India
Rupee	100 paisas	Pakistan
Rupee	100 pice	Nepal
Rouble	100 kopecks	Union of Soviet Socialist Republics
Rupiah	100 sen	Indonesia
Schilling	100 groschen	Austria
Shilling	100 cents	Kenya, Somali Republic, Tanzania, Uganda
Sol	100 centavos	Peru
Sucre	100 centavos	Ecuador
Taka	100 paise	Bangladesh
Tughrik	100 mongo	Mongolian People's Republic
Won	100 chon	South Korea
Won	100 jun	North Korea
Yen	100 sen	Japan
Yuan	100 cents	Republic of China (Taiwan)
Yuan	10 chiao	People's Republic of China
Zloty	100 groszy	Poland

MODIFIED GREAT STAFF

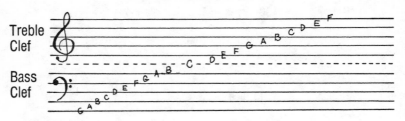

Treble Clef	
Bass Clef	

NOTE SYMBOLS		REST SYMBOLS	
Whole	o		▬
Half	♩		▬
Quarter	♩		⸴
Eighth	♪		𝄾
Sixteenth	♬		𝄿

KEY SIGNATURE AND TIME SIGNATURE

The Key Signature is placed at the head of the staff after the clef symbol, and indicates the necessary sharps (♯) or flats (♭) that will determine its tone.

The Time Signature follows the Key Signature, and tells the meter of the piece. The top number tells the number of beats per measure, and the bottom number tells the beat unit itself.

$\mathcal{N}$UTRITION INFORMATION

Essential Nutritional Elements

Protein — found in meat, fish, eggs and milk
Fats — found mainly in certain body tissues of animals and in
     some plants
Carbohydrates — found in starches and sugars
Vitamins — found in various foods
Minerals — found in various foods
Water

Four Basic Food Groups

Milk and Dairy Products
Breads and grains
Meat, poultry, fish, eggs (nuts and beans)
Fruits and vegetables

TWENTY-FIVE COMMON $\mathcal{P}$RODUCTS NOT IN USE FIFTY YEARS AGO

Air conditioning
Ball-point pens
Computers
Direct-dial telephones
Electric dishwasher
Electric garbage disposals
Fiber-glass
Films with sound and color
Homogenized milk
Instant photographs
Jet aircraft
Lasers
Micro-wave ovens

No-iron clothing
Office copy machines
Plastics
Pocket calculators
Power mowers
Satellites
Snow blowers
Space vehicles
Stereo recordings
Synthetic cloth
Television
Video tape recorders

Big Foot
a hurricane
the Abominable Snowman
a tornado
the Loch Ness Monster
a cyclone
Godzilla
a tidal wave
the Wicked Witch of the West
a volcanic eruption
Dracula
a landslide
Wolfman
an avalanche
Frankenstein
howls and other strange
    noises you can't identify
the Headless Horseman
thunder
the Hunchback of Notre Dame
lightning
the Bell Witch
darkness
Darth Vader
scalpings
witches
haunted houses
trolls
Mr. Hyde
footsteps behind you on
    a deserted street
dark caves
voodoo
being lost
black magic
a typhoon
war
a dust storm
warlocks
King Kong

fire and brimstone
sharks
barracudas
pyrannahs
snakes
spiders
alligators
crocodiles
things that go ''bump''
    in the night
Blackbeard
Captain Hook
Bluebeard
Jack the Ripper
the Boston Strangler
your first day of school
tests and exams
shots
Cinderella's wicked stepmother
Blackbeard the Pirate
giants
lions
tigers
bears
fires
explosions
goblins
wrecks
fog
UFO's
invaders from outer space
Tyrannosaurus Rex
ghosts
the Devil
poisons
dragons
octopuses
being tortured
earthquakes

Seven Wonders of the Ancient World

Name	Location
The Great Pyramid of King Khufu	Near Cairo, Egypt
The Hanging Gardens of Babylon by Nebuchadnezzar	Babylon
The Statue of Zeus by Phidias	Olympia, Greece
The Temple of Diana at Ephesus	Asia Minor
Mausoleum at Harlicarnassus (Tomb of King Mausolus)	Asia Minor
Colossus of Rhodes	Rhodes, (Ancient) Greece
Pharos of Alexandria (Harbor lighthouse)	Alexandria, Egypt

Signs and Symbols

WEATHER SYMBOLS

Cold Front		Warm Front	
Stationary Front		Squall Line	
Rain		Snow	✱
Hail	▲	Sleet	△
Frost	V	Fog	≡
Haze	∞	Thunder	T
Sheet Lightning	⟨	Thunderstorm	
No Cloud Cover (Clear)	○	One Quarter Cloud Cover	
One Half Cloud Cover	◐	Three Quarters Cloud Cover	
Completely Overcast	●	Calm Wind	◎
Wind (1-4 mph)	○—	Wind (15-20 mph)	
Wind (32-37 mph)		Wind (50-54 mph)	
High Pressure	ℍ	Low Pressure	𝕃

(cont.)

ASTRONOMY SYMBOLS

Earth

Jupiter

Mars

Mercury

Moon

Conjunction

Ascending Node,
Moon

Moon High

Neptune

Saturn

Sun

Venus

Uranus

Opposition

Descending Node,
Moon

Moon Low

ZODIAC SYMBOLS

Aquarius the Waterman (January 20 through February 18)

Pisces the Fish (February 19 through March 19)

Aries the Ram (March 20 through April 19)

Taurus the Bull (April 20 through May 20)

Gemini the Twins (May 21 through June 20)

Cancer the Crab (June 21 through July 22)

Leo the Lion (July 23 through August 22)

Virgo the Virgin (August 23 through September 22)

Libra the Reins (September 23 through October 22)

Scorpio the Scorpion (October 23 through November 21)

Sagitarrius the Archer (November 22 through December 21)

Capricorn the Goat (December 22 through January 19)

MAJOR BODIES OF OUR SOLAR SYSTEM

Name	How far from earth in miles (closest approach)	Length of Year (in earth days)	Average Temperature	Number of Satellites
Mercury	53,000,000	88	350°F 177°C	0
Venus	25,000,000	225	800°F 427°C	0
Earth		365	57°F 14°C	1
Mars	35,000,000	687	-80°F -62°C	2
Jupiter	390,000,000	4,333	Unknown—probably higher than -229°F -145°C	13
Saturn	793,000,000	10,759	Unknown—probably lower than -240°F -151°C	10
Uranus	1,700,000,000	30,685	Unknown—probably lower than -240°F -151°C	5
Neptune	2,678,000,000	60,188	Unknown—probably lower than -280°F -173°C	2
Pluto	2,700,000,000	90,700	Unknown—probably lower than -300°F -184°C	0

SPORTS AND GAMES

Acting Games
Anagrams
Archery
Auto Racing
Backgammon
Badminton
Baseball
Basketball
Bean Bag Toss
Bicycling
Billiards
Bingo
Board Games
Boating
Bobsledding
Bowling
Boxing
Bunt Ball
Canoeing
Card Games
Charades
Checkers
Chess
Chinese Checkers
Cricket
Croquet
Crossword Puzzles
Darts
Deck Tennis
Diving
Dodge Ball
Dominoes
Dot-to-dot Games
Electronic Games
Fencing
Field Hockey
Follow the Leader
Football
Golf
Guessing Games
Gymnastics
Handball
Hiking
Hockey
Hopscotch
Horseback Riding
Horseshoes

Hunting
I Spy
Ice Hockey
Ice Skating
Jacks
Jai Alai
Jogging
Jump Rope
Kickball
Kite Flying
La Crosse
Leap Frog
Mahjong
Marbles
Model Building
Paddle Tennis
Pin-the-tail ...
Ping Pong
Polo
Puzzles
Racing
Red Light
Rodeos
Riddles
Roller Skating
Rugby
Running
Sailing
Scrabble
Shuffleboard
Sledding
Skiing
Softball
Soccer
Squash
Straddle Ball
Swimming
Table Tennis
Tag
Target Games
Tennis
Tether Ball
Track & Field
Treasure Hunts
Tug-of-war
Volleyball
Wrestling

TELEPHONE NUMBERS TO LIST AND LEARN

Your Own _____

Your Parents (or Guardians) at Work

_____

_____

Other Family and/or Neighbors

_____

_____

_____

_____

Your School _____

Police Department _____

Fire Department_____

Your Doctor _____

Emergency _____

Library _____

Your Best Friend

_____

A Good Friend

_____

Another Good Friend

_____

Tongue Twisters

Frank found forty-four flavorful frankfurters.

The gray goose gladly grazed in the green grass.

Carrie Clark, Clara Clark, Cora Clark

Eleven elegant elephants ate lettuce, eggs and leeks.

Six slim, slick, silver saplings.

He bristled when a missent missle twisted his thistles.

A sheet slitter stealthily slits sheets.

Mable might mix six musty milled sticks.

She sells seashells by the seashore.

The shortstop stopped short and shot singles slowly.

A bitter biting blast bashed the bouncing boat.

How much wood would a woodchuck chuck if a woodchuck could chuck wood?

She sipped cider sodas through thin, striped straws.

The dumb bum stumbled under the crumpled bundle.

The querulous king quarreled quietly with his quivering queen.

See Pamela proudly posing, supposing her pose is imposing.

Will that shop stock shirts and short socks?

Did cross Ross rush across the frosty moss?

Tom tried twice to tie the tie. On the third try, he tied it in a trice.

The belligerent bricklayer broke the back black brick.

He stuck silver slivers in the slatted stilts.

TOOLS

... for the Artist

drawing paper	drawing pencils	chalk & charcoal
water colors	oil paints	assorted brushes
canvass	turpentine or	easel
smock	linseed oil	palette

... for the Gardener

hoe	shovel	clipper
trowel	string	marker
stakes	gloves	hose
black plastic	pruning shears	rake

... for the Handyman

hammer	screwdriver	Phillips-head
assorted nails	wrench	screwdriver
saw	hacksaw	pliers
assorted screws	ruler	drill and bits
tool box	sandpaper	carpenter's pencils

... for the Kitchen

measuring spoon	measuring cup	mixing bowls
wooden spoons	sharp knives	parer
carrot scraper	sieve	strainer
collander	pots, pans & tops	hand mixer
chopping board	grater	pot holders
sifter	whisk	spatula
funnel	timer	spoon rest

... for the Student

paper	pencils	pens
erasers	crayons	pencil sharpener
notebooks	dictionary	thesaurus
ruler	compass	protractor
scissors	paper clips	library card
cellophane tape	scratch paper	glue

U.S. CABINET POSTS

Department of State ....Secretary of State
Treasury Department ....Secretary of the Treasury
Department of Defense ....Secretary of Defense
Department of Justice ....Attorney General
Department of Interior ....Secretary of the Interior
Department of Agriculture...............Secretary of Agriculture
Department of Commerce and Labor ....Secretary of Commerce and
Secretary of Labor
Department of Education.................Secretary of Education
Department of Health and Human Services ....Secretary of
Health and Human Services
Department of Housing
and Urban Development ....Secretary of Housing and
Secretary of Urban Development
Department of Transportation ....Secretary of Transportation
Department of Energy ....Secretary of Energy

HIGHLIGHTS OF U.S. HISTORY

Event	Date
Christopher Columbus Lands in America	1492
Mayflower Compact (First Plan of Government)	November 21, 1620
Pilgrims Land and Settle at Plymouth	December 25, 1620
Poor Richard's Almanac — First Publication	1733
French and Indian War	1754-1760
Stamp Act	March 22, 1765
Boston Tea Party	December 16, 1773
Revolutionary War	1775-1783
Declaration of Independence	July 4, 1776
Ratification of Articles of Confederation	March 1, 1781
Ratification of Constitution	March 4, 1789
Washington's Inauguration	April 30, 1789
Louisiana Purchase	April 30, 1803
War of 1812	1812-1814
Monroe Doctrine	December 2, 1823

(cont.)

Discovery of Gold in California	January 24, 1848
Mexican War	1846-1848
Civil War	1861-1865
Emancipation Proclamation	January 1, 1863
Abraham Lincoln Assassinated	April 14, 1865
Spanish-American War	1898
First Airplane Flight	December 17, 1903
World War I (US Entrance to End)	1917-1918
Stock Market Crash	1929
New Deal Begins	March 9, 1933
World War II (US Entrance to End)	1941-1945
Founding of the United Nations (First Session of the General Assembly)	January 10, 1946
Korean War	1950-1953
First American in Space	May 5, 1961
Vietnam War	1961-1973
Cuban Missle Crisis	1962
John F. Kennedy Assassinated	November 22, 1963
Civil Rights Act	July 2, 1964
Richard M. Nixon Resigned	August 9, 1974
Launching of Voyager II	August 20, 1977
Mt. St. Helens Eruptions	1980

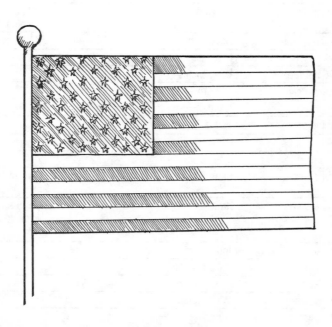

NOTEWORTHY VOLCANOES

Name	Location	Eruption Dates	Notes
Ajusco	Mexico	1952-1953	
Anak Krakatoa	Indonesia	1927, 1969	
Aniakchak	Alaska	1923, 1931	
Ararat	Turkey		extinct
Aso	Japan	1970	world's largest crater
Chimborazo	Ecuador		
Cotopaxi	Ecuador		50 eruptions between 1742 and 1942
El Boqueron or Barcena Volcano	San Benedicto Island off Mexico	1952-1953	
El Misti	Peru		
Eldfell	island off Iceland	1973	
Galunggung	Java	1822, 1918	
Hekla	Iceland	1970	
Hibokhibok	Philippines	1951	
Kelud	Java	1919, 1967	
Kilauea	Hawaii	1823-1924, 1971	
Kilimanjaro	Tanzania		extinct; highest volcano in Africa
Klyuchevskoi	Soviet Union	1700-1966	72 eruptions
Krakatoa	Indonesia	1883	
La Soufriere	West Indies	1902, 1956	
Lassen Peak	California	1914-1921	
Laki	Iceland	1783	
Lamington	Papua New Guinea	1951	
Makian	Halmahera	1760	
Manam	Melanesia	1814	
Mauna Kea	Hawaii	1952-1953	highest island peak in world
Mauna Loa	Hawaii		world's largest volcanic structure
Mt. Agung	Indonesia	1963, 1964	
Mt. Apo	Philippine Islands		
Mt. Asama	Japan	1965	very frequent
Mt. Baker	Washington, U.S.		
Mt. Cameroon	Africa		

Name	Location	Eruption Dates	Notes
Mt. Etna	Sicily	122 A.D. 1669,1886, 1910,1928, 1950,1964, 1971,1974	largest in Europe
Mt. Fuji	Japan		inactive; highest in Japan
Mt. Hood	Oregon, U.S.		inactive
Mt. Katmai	Aleutian Islands, U.S.	1912, 1931	
Mt. Pelee	Martinique	1902, 1929-1932	
Mt. Rainier	Washington, U.S.		
Mt. St. Helens	Washington, U.S.	1980	
Mt. Tambora	Indonesia	1815	
Nyamuragira	Africa	1971	
Nyiragongo	Africa		active since 1935
Orizaba	Mexico	1687	
Papandayan	Java	1772, 1925	
Paricutin	Mexico	1943, 1952	
Pichincha	Ecuador	1881	
Popocatepetl	Mexico	1920	
Sakurajima	Japan	1914, 1972	almost always active
Stromboli	island in Mediterra-nean	1930, 1971	continuous activity
Surtsey	North Atlantic Ocean	1963-1967	
Taal	Philippines	1911, 1969	
Ternate	Indonesia	from 1538-1963	50 eruptions
Thira	Santorin; Mediterra-nean Sea	1950	1300's B.C.; may have caus-ed the loss of the fabled city of Atlantis
Unzen dake	Japan	1792	
Vesuvius	Italy	A.D. 79, 1631, 1779, 1872, 1906, 1911-1944	

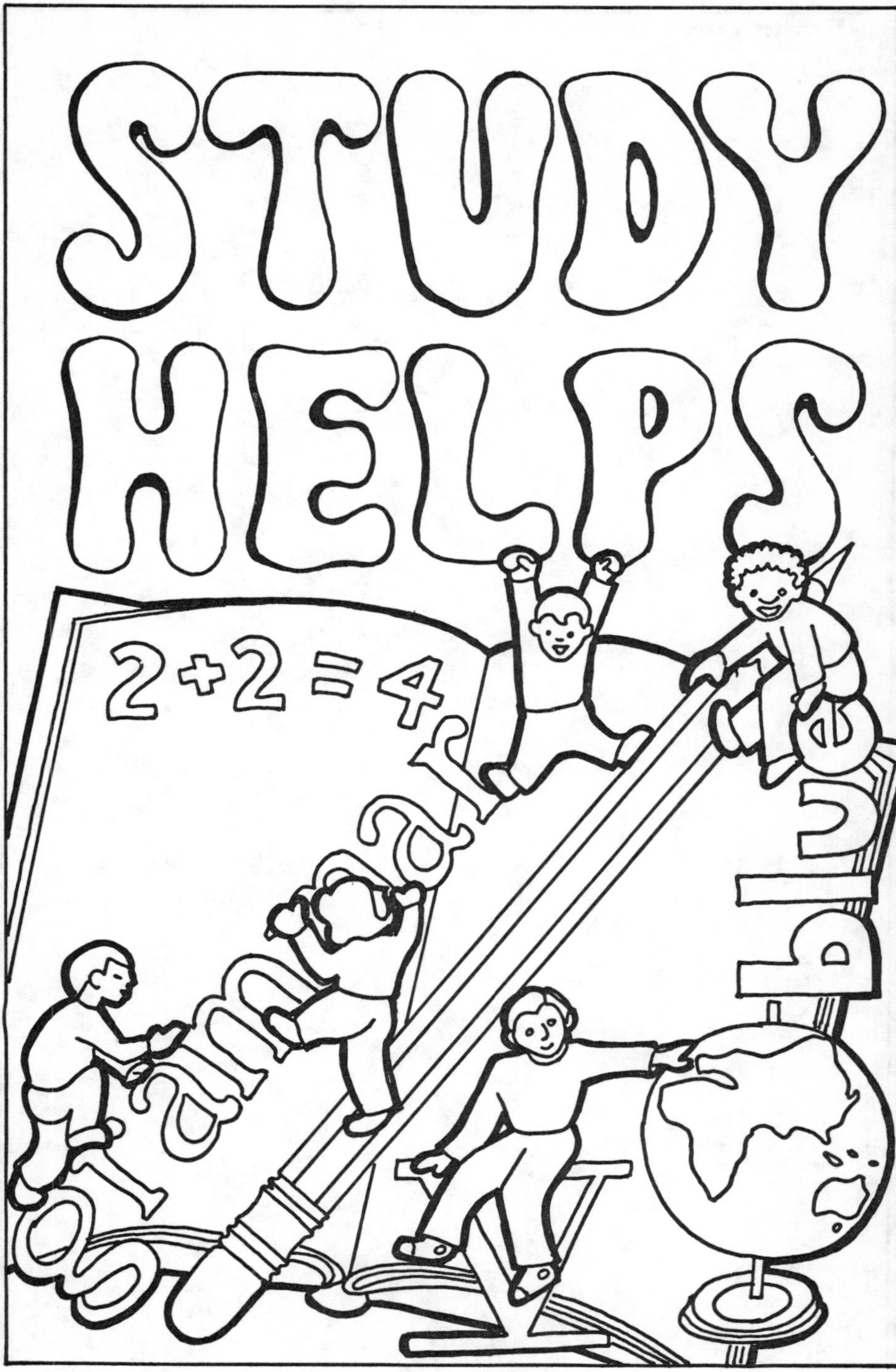
STUDY
HELPS
2+2=4
blue

YOUR LIST

ℬBBREVIATIONS

A.D.	Anno Domini, in the year of our Lord
A.M., a.m.	ante meridiem, before noon
Amer.	America; American
anon.	anonymous
assn.	association
asst.	assistant
ave.	avenue
B.C.	Before Christ
B.C.E.	Before the Common Era
bibliog.	bibliography
bldg.	building
blvd.	boulevard
C	Centigrade; Celcius
cap.	capital
cent.	century
ch., chap.	chapter
cm.	centimeter
c/o	care of
co.	company, county
c.o.d.	cash on delivery
conf.	conference
cont.	continued
coop.	cooperative
corp.	corporation
C.S.T.	Central Standard Time
dept.	department
diag.	diagram
dm.	decimeter
doz.	dozen
D.S.T.	Daylight Saving Time
ed.	edition
elem.	elementary
Eng.	English
E.S.T.	Eastern Standard Time
etc.	et cetera, and so forth
F	Fahrenheit
fig.	figure
Fri.	Friday
ft.	feet; foot; fort
gal.	gallon
geog.	geography
Gov.	Governor

——— (cont.) ———

govt.	government
gr.	gram
hr.	hour
ht.	height
I., i.	island
ibid.	ibidem, in the same place
ill., illus.	illustration
inc.	incorporated
in.	inch
intro.	introduction
I.O.U.	I owe you
I.Q.	intelligence quotient
Jr.	Junior
junc.	junction
kg.	kilogram
km.	kilometer
l.	liter
lab.	laboratory
lang.	language
lat.	latitude
lb.	pound
lib.	library
lit.	literature
Lieut., Lt.	Lieutenant
long.	longitude
Ltd., Lim.	Limited
m.	meter
max.	maximum
mdse.	merchandise
memo	memorandum
mfr., manuf.	manufacturer
min.	minute; minimum
misc.	miscellaneous
mi.	mile
mml.	millimeter
mo.	month
Mon.	Monday
mph	miles per hour
Mr.	Mister
Mrs.	Mistress
Ms.	Miss or Mrs.
M.S.T.	Mountain Standard Time
Mt., mt.	mount; mountain
nat., natl.	national

no.	number
oz.	ounce
p.	page
par.	paragraph; parenthesis
pd.	paid
phot.	photograph
pl.	plural
P.M., p.m.	post meridiem; after noon
P.O.	post office
pop.	population
ppd.	prepaid
prin.	principal
P.S.	post scriptum; postscript
P.S.T.	Pacific Standard Time
pt.	pint
qt.	quart
rd.	road
ref.	reference; refer
reg.	region; regulation
R.S.V.P.	Answer, if you please
Sat.	Saturday
secy.	secretary
sig.	signature
sing.	singular
sp.	spelling
sq.	square
Sr.	Senior
St.	saint; street
subj.	subject
Sun.	Sunday
Supt.	Superintendent
t.	ton
temp.	temperature
Thurs.	Thursday
treas.	treasurer
Tues.	Tuesday
v, vs	versus; against
vol.	volume
Wed.	Wednesday
wk.	week
wt.	weight
yd.	yard
yr.	year

ACRONYMS

An acronym *is a word formed from the initial letters of a name and pronounced as a word. Here are some selected acronyms.*

ASCAP — American Society of Composers, Authors and Publishers
AWOL — Absent With Out Leave
CARE — Cooperative for American Remittances Everywhere
CORE — Congress of Racial Equality
DOVAP — Doppler Velocity and Position
HUD — (Department of) Housing and Urban Development
NASA — National Aeronautics and Space Administration
NATO — North Atlantic Treaty Organization
NOW — National Organization of Women
radar — radio detecting and ranging
rem — Roentgen Equivalent in Man
SHAPE — Supreme Headquarters, Allied Command, Europe
snafu — situation normal - all fouled up
UNICEF — United Nations International Children's Fund
WAAC — Women's Army Auxiliary Corps
WAAF — Women's Auxiliary Air Force
WAC — Women's Army Corps
WAF — Women in the Air Force
WAVES — Women Accepted for Volunteer Emergency Service

CAPITALIZATION USAGE

Capitalize the first letter in:
1. The first word of a sentence.
2. The first word in each line of poetry.
3. The first and all other important words in the greeting of a letter.
4. The first word in the closing of a letter.
5. The first, last, and other main words in titles of chapters, stories, poems, reports, songs, books, movies, and radio and television programs.
6. The word *I*.
7. A proper adjective.
8. Initials.
9. Titles of persons (Mr., Ms., Mrs., Dr.).
10. Abbreviations (P.O., R.R., C.O.D., Dr.)
11. Titles of high government officials.
12. A proper noun.
13. Words like Mother, Sister, Uncle when used in place of or with names.

——— (cont.) ———

── **CAPITALIZATION USAGE** (cont.) ──

14. Names of schools, clubs, organizations and buildings.
15. Names of streets, avenues, boulevards, roads and Rural Route.
16. Names of cities, towns, counties, states, countries and continents.
17. Names of rivers, oceans, mountains and regions (the South).
18. Names of days, months, holidays and other special days.
19. Names of businesses and special products.
20. Names of languages, nationalities and special groups.
21. Names of political parties.
22. Names of government departments.
23. Names for the Deity.
24. Names of churches and religious denominations.
25. Names of historical events and documents.
26. Names of airlines, ships and railroads.
27. Names of magazines and newspapers.
28. The first word of a head and a subhead in outlines.
29. The first word after a strong interjection.

── **COLORS** ──

Primary and Secondary Colors in Paint
Primary: BLUE, RED, YELLOW
Secondary : GREEN, ORANGE, VIOLET
The Secondary colors are produced by mixing the Primary colors as follows:
Blue plus Red equals Violet
Blue plus Yellow equals Green
Red plus Yellow equals Orange
All other colors are made by mixing the above in various combinations and proportions. Hues and tints are created by adding white and/or black. For example:
Red plus White equals Pink
Violet plus White equals Lavendar
Orange plus Black equals Cinnamon
Red plus White plus Black equals Rose

Primary Colors in Light
BLUE, GREEN, RED
All other colors in the spectrum are made by various combinations of the above three primary colors. When combined equally, the primary colors produce white light.

COMPOUND WORDS

afternoon
airplane
anybody
anyone
anyplace
anything
anytime
anyway
anywhere
arrowhead
backbone
backyard
baseball
basketball
bathrobe
bathroom
bathtub
bedroom
bedtime
beehive
birdbath
blackboard
blacksmith
boathouse
broomstick
buckskin
butterfly
campfire
campground
candlestick
cannot
catfish
chairman
checkerboard
cheeseburger
classmate
classroom
coastline
coffeepot
commonplace
corncob
cornfield

countryside
courthouse
courtyard
cowboy
craftsman
crossbow
daybreak
dishpan
doorbell
doorway
downhill
downstairs
downstream
downtown
driftwood
driveway
drugstore
dugout
earthquake
eggshell
elsewhere
everybody
everyone
everything
everywhere
eyebrow
eyelid
farewell
farmhouse
fingerprint
fireman
fireworks
flagpole
flashlight
flowerpot
football
footprint
framework
freshman
furthermore
gingerbread
grandfather

grandmother
grassland
hairbrush
halfway
handshake
headdress
headline
highlands
highway
hillside
homeland
homemade
homework
hopscotch
horseback
horseshoe
hourglass
houseboat
household
however
icebox
indoor
inland
inside
into
junkyard
landmark
lifetime
lighthouse
lightweight
lookout
lowlands
mailbox
mainland
moonlight
mountainside
newspaper
nightfall
nobody
northeast
notebook
nothing

nowhere
otherwise
outcome
outdoors
outline
outside
overcome
overhead
overlook
overnight
paintbrush
pancake
playground
policeman
popcorn
quarterback
raincoat
raindrop
railroad
rattlesnake
roadside
rowboat
runway
sailboat
salesman
scarecrow
schoolhouse
schoolroom
scrapbook
seaport
seashell
seashore
seaweed
sidewalk
snowflake
snowman
somebody
someday
somehow
someone
something
sometime

(cont.)

COMPOUND WORDS (cont.)

somewhere	sunshine	warehouse
southwest	textbook	waterfall
spaceship	themselves	weekend
springtime	thereafter	whatever
stagecoach	townspeople	whenever
stairway	treetop	wherever
starfish	undergo	widespread
steamboat	underground	wildlife
storekeeper	underline	windmill
summertime	underside	within
sundown	underwater	without
sunlight	upright	woodland
sunrise	upstream	worthwhile
sunset	vineyard	yourself

DIVISIONS OF THE DEWEY DECIMAL SYSTEM

000 — GENERALITIES
010 - Bibliographies & Catalogs
020 - Library Science
030 - General Encyclopedic Works
040 - (NA)
050 - General Periodicals
060 - General Organizations
070 - Newspapers and Journalism
080 - General Collections
090 - Manuscripts and Book Rarities

100 — PHILOSOPHY AND RELATED
110 - Ontology and Methodology
120 - Knowledge, Cause, Purpose and Man
130 - Pseudo- and Parapsychology
140 - Specific Philosophic Viewpoints
150 - Psychology
160 - Logic
170 - Ethics (Moral Philosophy)
180 - Ancient, Med. and Oriental Philosophies
190 - Modern Western Philosophy

(cont.)

200 — RELIGION
210 - Natural Religion
220 - Bible
230 - Christian Doctrinal Theology
240 - Christian Moral and Devotional Theology
250 - Christian Pastoral, Parochial, etc.
260 - Christian Social and Eccles. Theology
270 - History and Geog. of Christ. Church
280 - Christian Denominations and Sects
290 - Other Religions; Comparative Religions

300 — SOCIAL SCIENCES
310 - Statistical Method and Statistics
320 - Political Science
330 - Economics
340 - Law
350 - Public Administration
360 - Welfare and Association
370 - Education
380 - Commerce
390 - Customs and Folklore

400 — LANGUAGE
410 - Linguistics and Nonverbal Language
420 - English and Anglo-Saxon
430 - Germanic Languages
440 - French, Provencal, Catalan
450 - Italian, Romanian, etc.
460 - Spanish and Portuguese
470 - Italic Languages
480 - Classical and Greek
490 - Other Languages

500 — PURE SCIENCES
510 - Mathematics
520 - Astronomy and Allied Sciences
530 - Physics
540 - Chemistry and Allied Sciences
550 - Earth Sciences
560 - Paleontology
570 - Anthropological and Biological Sciences
580 - Botanical Sciences
590 - Zoological Sciences

600 — TECHNOLOGY
610 - Medical Sciences
620 - Engineering and Allied Operations
630 - Agriculture and Agric. Industries
640 - Domestic Arts & Sciences
650 - Business and Related Enterprises
660 - Chemical Technology (etc.)
670 - Manufactures Processible
680 - Assembled and Final Products
690 - Buildings

700 — THE ARTS
710 - Civic and Landscape Art
720 - Architecture
730 - Sculpture and the Plastic Arts
740 - Drawing and Decorative Arts
750 - Painting and Paintings
760 - Graphic Arts
770 - Photography and Photographs
780 - Music
790 - Recreation (Recreational Arts)

800 — LITERATURE AND RHETORIC
810 - American Literature in English
820 - English/Anglo-Saxon Literature
830 - Germanic Languages Literature
840 - French, Provencal, Catalan Literature
850 - Italian, Romanian (etc.) Literature
860 - Spanish and Portuguese Literature
870 - Italic Languages Literature
880 - Classical and Greek Literature
890 - Literature of Other Languages

900 — GENERAL GEOGRAPHY AND HISTORY
910 - General Geography
920 - General Biography, Genealogy, etc.
930 - General History of Ancient World
940 - General History of Modern Europe
950 - General History of Modern Asia
960 - General History of Modern Africa
970 - General History of North America
980 - General History of South America
990 - General History of Rest of World

ABSTRACT NOUN—a noun that names something that does not have a physical substance. *Example: compassion.*

ACTIVE VOICE—a verb which expresses action and can take a direct object. *Example:* I *threw* the ball.

ADJECTIVE—a word that modifies a noun or a pronoun. *Example:* the *white* ball.

ADVERB—a word that modifies a verb, an adjective, or another adverb. *Example:* Go *slowly.*

ANTECENDENT—the word, phrase, or clause to which a relative pronoun refers. A pronoun must agree with its antecendent in number. *Example:* Erin gave me *his* ball.

ARTICLES—the adjectives *a, an,* and *the.*

AUXILIARY VERB—a verb that accompanies another verb to show tense, mood, or voice. *Example:* She *has* gone.

CLAUSE—a group of words that contains a subject and a predicate, and forms part of a compound or complex sentence. *Example: After I left, she called.*

COLLECTIVE NOUN—a noun that denotes a collection of persons or things regarded as a unit; usually takes a singular verb. *Example:* The *committee* chooses its own chairman.

COMMON NOUN—a noun that indicates any one of a class of persons, places, or things. *Example: boy; town; ball.*

COMPARATIVE ADJECTIVE—an adjective form (ending in —er or adding the word *more* before the word) used when two person or things are compared. *Example:* This apple is *smaller* and *more delicious* than that one.

COMPLEX SENTENCE—a sentence containing one independent clause and one or more dependent clauses. *Example: I went to town to shop, but found that all the stores were closed.*

COMPOUND SENTENCE—a sentence containing two or more independent clauses joined by a conjunction. *Example: I called my friend, and we talked for an hour.*

COMPOUND-COMPLEX SENTENCE—a sentence that has two or more independent clauses and at least one dependent or subordinate clause. *Example: When she opened the door, there was no one on the porch, and the street was empty, too.*

CONCRETE NOUN—a noun that names a physical, visible, or tangible item. *Example: airplane.*

CONJUNCTION—a word that connects words, phrases, or clauses. *Example:* I like toast *and* jam.

COORDINATING CONJUNCTION—a conjunction used to connect two independent clauses. *Example:* He grinned, *and* I giggled.

CORRELATIVE CONJUNCTIONS—conjunctions which are used in pairs. *Example: Neither* Alan *nor* Amy will go.

DEPENDENT (OR SUBORDINATE) CLAUSE—a clause that functions as a noun, adjective, or adverb within a sentence, but cannot stand alone. *Example: What she said* was true.

DIRECT OBJECT—the noun, pronoun, or noun phrase in a sentence which receives the action of a transitive verb. *Example:* I threw the *ball.*

GERUND—a verb form ending in -ing, usually used as a noun. *Example: Skiing* is fun.

INDEFINITE PRONOUN—a pronoun that does not specify the identity of its object. *Example: Anyone* can come.

INDEPENDENT CLAUSE—a clause which contains at least a subject and a predicate, and is capable of standing alone. *Example: I went to the store.*

INDIRECT OBJECT—the noun, pronoun, or noun phrase named as the one to or for whom action involving a direct object is done. *Example:* He threw *me* the ball.

INFINITIVE—a non-inflected verb form usually preceeded by *to,* used as a noun, adjective, or adverb. *Example: To run* fast is fun.

INTENSIVE PRONOUN—a pronoun which is used for emphasis. *Example:* I *myself* saw it.

INTERJECTION—an exclamatory word or phrase. *Example: Hey! Look out!*

INTRANSITIVE VERB—a verb that cannot take an object. *Example:* She *learns* easily.

LINKING VERB—a verb that can be followed by an adjective that modifies the subject. *Example:* Randy *is* tall.

MODIFY—to qualify or limit the meaning of. *Example: very* small.

NOUN—a word that names a person, place, or thing. *Examples: girl; city; hat.*

PARAGRAPH—a distinct division within a written work that may consist of several sentences or just one, that expresses something relevant to the whole work but is complete within itself. The first word of a paragraph is almost always indented.

PASSIVE VOICE—a verb which expresses state of being and cannot take a direct object. *Example:* He *was asked* to leave.

(cont.)

PAST TENSE—a verb form that expresses action or condition that occurred in the past. *Example:* Yesterday I *went* to town.

PERSONAL PRONOUN—a pronoun that denotes the speaker, person spoken to, or person spoken about. *Example: You* can find it.

POSITIVE ADJECTIVE—an adjective form used to assign a quality to the word it modifies. *Example:* the *fast* car.

POSSESSIVE PRONOUN—a pronoun that shows possession. *Example:* That car is *mine.*

PREDICATE—the portion of a sentence or clause that tells something about the subject, consisting of a verb and possibly including objects, modifiers, and/or verb complements. *Example:* Margaret *was here.*

PREDICATE ADJECTIVE—an adjective that refers to, describes, or limits the subject of a sentence. *Example:* The rock is *heavy.*

PREDICATE NOMINATIVE—a noun following a form of the verb *to be* in a sentence which modifies the subject. *Example:* She is *Alicia.*

PREPOSITION—a word that shows relationship (often between verbs and nouns or nouns and nouns) and takes an object. *Example:* Put it *on* the table.

PREPOSITIONAL PHRASE—a group of words in a sentence that includes a preposition and its object, along with any modifiers of the object. *Example:* Put it *on the first table.*

PRESENT TENSE—a verb form that expresses current time. *Example:* I *am* here.

PRONOUN—a word that takes the place of a noun. *Example: I; you; she; it; he.*

PROPER NOUN—a noun that names a particular person, place, or thing, and is capitalized. *Examples: Omaha; Jenny.*

REFLEXIVE PRONOUN—a pronoun that ends in -self or -selves; used to point the action back to the subject. *Example:* You will hurt *yourself.*

RELATIVE PRONOUN—a pronoun that shows a relationship. *Example:* It was he *who* did it.

RUN-ON (OR FUSED) SENTENCE—a sentence in which two complete sentences are run together with no punctuation to separate them. (Run-on sentences are not acceptable in standard written English.) *Example: I went to the movie I ate some popcorn.*

── (cont.) ──

GRAMMAR ''GOODIES'' (cont.)

SENTENCE—a basic unit of language which must contain a subject and a predicate. *Example: I went to the movie.*

SUBJECT—a word or phrase in a sentence that is the doer of the action, or receives the action (in passive voice), or which is described; must agree in number with the predicate. *Example: Margaret* was there.

SUBJUNCTIVE (OR CONDITIONAL) MOOD—a set of verb forms used to express contingent or hypothetical action, usually introduced by *if, that,* etc., and always taking the plural form of the verb. *Example: If I were you,* I'd go.

SUPERLATIVE ADJECTIVE—an adjective form (ending in *—est* or adding the word *most* before the word) used when three or more things are involved in a comparison. *Example:* This is the *slowest* of all cars.

TRANSITIVE VERB—a verb which can take an object within a sentence. *Example:* He *threw* the ball.

VERB—a word that shows action, state of being, or occurrence. *Examples: run; is; find.*

From: THE YELLOW PAGES FOR STUDENTS & TEACHERS by the KIDS' STUFF People. Copyright © 1979 by Incentive Publications, Inc. Used by permission.

GOOD STUDY HABITS

- Make a work schedule for each day.
- Make sure your supplies are in order.
- Keep your work area neat.
- Listen carefully when assignments are made.
- Ask good, well thought-out questions.
- Check your work for accuracy in spelling and punctuation.
- Recopy your work when necessary.
- Use your dictionary and other study helps regularly.
- Use good organizational skills.
- Finish your work on time.
- Make good use of the library.

Printed Alphabet

Aa Bb Cc Dd

Ee Ff Gg Hh

Ii Jj Kk Ll

Mm Nn Oo

Pp Qq Rr Ss

Tt Uu Vv Ww

Xx Yy Zz

Cursive Alphabet

Aa Bb Cc Dd

Ee Ff Gg Hh

Ii Jj Kk Ll

Mm Nn Oo

Pp Qq Rr Ss

Tt Uu Vv Ww

Xx Yy Zz

MATH SYMBOLS

+	add	>	greater than
∠	angle	∩	intersection (of sets)
⌢	arc	<	less than
2_5	base 5 numeral	——	line segment
≅	congruent	x	multiply
•	decimal point	-2	negative integer
°C	degrees Celsius	π	pi (3.14 or 22/7)
°F	degrees Farenheit	+2	positive integer
⌐ or ÷	divide	—→	ray
∅	empty set	√	square root
=	equal	-	subtract
≈	equivalent	≠	unequal
3^3	exponential number (3x3x3)	≉	unequivalent
¼	fraction	⌣	union (of sets)

MEASUREMENT HELPS

12 inches = 1 foot
3 feet = 1 yard
5,280 feet and 1,760 yards = 1 mile
4,840 square yards and 43,560 square feet = 1 acre

16 ounces = 1 pound
2000 pounds = 1 ton

KITCHEN MEASUREMENT HELPS

3 teaspoons = 1 tablespoon
2 tablespoons = 1 ounce
8 ounces = 1 cup
2 cups = 1 pint
2 pints = 1 quart
4 quarts = 1 gallon

1/4 teaspoon = 1.25 milliliters
1/2 teaspoon = 2.5 milliliters
3/4 teaspoon = 3.75 milliliters
1 teaspoon = 5 milliliters

1/4 tablespoon = 3.75 milliliters
1/2 tablespoon = 7.5 milliliters
3/4 tablespoon = 11.25 milliliters
1 tablespoon = 15 milliliters

1/4 cup = 59 milliliters
1/3 cup = 79 milliliters
1/2 cup = 118 milliliters
2/3 cup = 157 milliliters
3/4 cup = 177 milliliters
1 cup = 236 milliliters

1/2 pint = 237 milliliters
1 pint = 473 milliliters
1 quart = 946.3 milliliters
1 gallon = 3785 milliliters

1/4 ounce = 7.09 grams
1/2 ounce = 14.17 grams
3/4 ounce = 21.26 grams
1 ounce = 28.35 grams

METAPHORS

A metaphor is a figure of speech in which one thing is compared to another to suggest that they are similar.

My mind is a kingdom to me. (Shakespeare)
Reason is the life of the law. (Shakespeare)
All the world's a stage.... (Shakespeare)
The world is my oyster. (Shakespeare)
Our doubts are traitors. (Shakespeare)
It is meat and drink to me. (Shakespeare)
How sharper than a serpent's tooth it is/To have a thankless
    child. (Shakespeare)
Man is his own star.... (Fletcher)
Bread is the staff of life. (Swift)
Our birth is but a sleep and a forgetting.... (Wordsworth)
Friendship is Love without his wings. (Byron)
A thing of beauty is a joy forever. (Keats)
Beauty is truth, truth beauty.... (Keats)
Blossomed the lovely stars, the forget-me-nots of the angels.
    (Longfellow)
Literature is the thought of thinking souls. (Carlyle)
A babe in a house is a well-spring of pleasure. (Tupper)

Metric Conversions

English Unit		Approximate Metric Equivalent
inch	=	2.54 centimeters
foot	=	30.48 centimeters
yard	=	.91 meters
mile	=	1.6 kilometers
square inch	=	6.45 square centimeters
square foot	=	.09 square meters
square yard	=	.84 square meters
square mile	=	2.59 square kilometers
acre	=	4047.00 square meters
cubic inch	=	16.39 cubic centimeters
cubic foot	=	.03 cubic meters
cubic yard	=	.76 cubic meters
ounce	=	28.35 grams
pound	=	.45 kilograms
ton	=	.9 metric tons
pint	=	.47 liters
quart	=	.95 liters
gallon	=	3.78 liters
bushel	=	35.23 liters

Oxymorons

An oxymoron *is any combination of contradictory words that creates an epigrammatic effect. Here are some examples.*

a wise fool	quiet thunder
the happy pessimist	a tiny giant
poor little rich kid	a loud whisper
a sad smile	the beginning of the end
a valiant coward	happy tears
hiding in plain sight	an uneasy calm

OUTLINE FORMAT

I. _____

   A. _____

      1. _____

      2. _____

         a. _____

         b. _____

   B. _____

   C. _____

II. _____

   A. _____

   B. _____

      1. _____

      2. _____

   C. _____

   D. _____

      1. _____

         a. _____

         b. _____

      2. _____

III. _____

PALINDROMES

A palindrome is a word, phrase, sentence or number which reads exactly the same both forward and backward. Here are some examples.

radar	noon
pop	pup
mom	level
dad	rotor
not a ton	wet stew
Was it a cat I saw?	Madam, I'm Adam.
737	98289

PERSONIFICATIONS

A personification is a statement in which a thing or quality is represented in human form.

How sweet the moonlight sleeps upon this bank! (Shakespeare)

The inaudible and noiseless foot of time. (Shakespeare)

I will instruct my sorrows to be proud. (Shakespeare)

We cannot hold mortality's strong hand. (Shakespeare)

Truth hath a quiet breast. (Shakespeare)

I talk of dreams, which are the children of an idle brain. (Shakespeare)

Brevity is the soul of wit. (Shakespeare)

Ingratitude, thou marble-hearted fiend. (Shakespeare)

(cont.)

Patience, thou young and rose-lipp'd cherubin. (Shakespeare)

That old bald cheater, Time (Jonson)

Honest labor bears a lovely face. (Dekker)

Death was now armed with a new terror. (Miner)

Music's golden tongue/Flatter'd to tears this aged man and poor. (Keats)

And thou, vast ocean! on whose awful face/Time's iron fist can print no ruin-trace. (Montgomery)

For time will teach thee soon the truth ... (Longfellow)

To crack the voice of Melody/And break the legs of Time ...(Holmes)

PROBLEM SPELLING WORDS

accept	coming	existence
accommodate	commit	experience
acknowledgment	commitment	explanation
acquaintance	committed	extension
across	committee	February
affect	confident	foreign
already	conscientious	fourth
among	controversy	government
analysis	convenient	grammar
apparent	criticism	guarantee
appearance	description	height
arrangement	difference	immediately
attendance	disappoint	incidentally
begin	effect	inconvenience
beginning	eligible	its
benefit	endeavor	judgment
benefited	equipped	knowledgeable
business	especially	laboratory
calendar	exceed	loose
canceled	except	maintenance

(cont.)

PROBLEM SPELLING WORDS (cont.)

manila	principal	similar
necessary	principle	simile
oblige	privilege	sincerely
occasion	procedure	stationary
occurred	proceed	stationery
omission	probably	strictly
omitted	questionnaire	their
opportunity	really	there
original	receive	too
pamphlet	recommend	undoubtedly
personal	refer	unnecessary
personnel	reference	using
possession	referred	Wednesday
practical	referring	weather
practically	schedule	whether

PROOFREADS' MARKS

Mark	Explanation
¶	begin new paragraph
(Cap)	make capital
(lc)	make lower case
∧	insert
∧,	insert comma
∧.	insert period
⌒	close up space
ℓ	delete
∨̇	insert apostrophe
(sp)	spell out or spell correctly
∨̈ / ∨̈	insert quotation marks

130

A stitch in time saves nine.

More haste, less speed.

An apple a day keeps the doctor away.

Birds in their little nest agree.

Early to bed, early to rise, makes a man healthy, wealthy and
wise.

Whatever is worth doing at all is worth doing well.

Take care of the pence, for the pounds will take care of
themselves.

Never leave that till tomorrow which you can do today.

Little strokes fell great oaks.

He that goes a-borrowing goes a-sorrowing.

Remember that time is money.

There never was a good war or a bad peace.

Nothing is certain but death and taxes.

The pen is mightier than the sword.

It matters not how a man dies, but how he lives.

The road to Hell is paved with good intentions.

Silence gives consent.

Ask me no questions and I'll tell you no fibs.

Handsome is that handsome does.

Truth is stranger than fiction.

Variety's the very spice of life.

Haste maketh waste.

Of two evils, the less is always to be chosen.

By uniting we stand, by dividing we fall.

'Tis better to have loved and lost than never to have loved at all.

Necessity is the mother of invention.

Tall oaks from little acorns grow.

The child is father of the man.

Distance lends enchantment.

All things come round to him who will but wait.

Be it ever so humble, there's no place like home.

A thing of beauty is a joy forever.

Beauty is truth; truth beauty — that is all ye know on earth, and
all ye need to know.

Love is blind.

All that glisters is not gold.

Men have died from time to time, and worms have eaten them —
but not for love.

The ripest fruit falls first.

Cowards die many times before their deaths;/The valiant never
taste of death but once.

PUNCTUATION USAGE

A **period** is used:
1. At the end of a declarative sentence.
2. At the end of an imperative sentence.
3. After numerals and letters in outlines.
4. At the end of a business request stated in question form.
5. After an abbreviation or an initial.

A **question mark** is used:
1. At the end of an interrogative sentence.
2. Inside parentheses after a date or statement to show doubt.

An **exclamation point** is used:
1. At the end of an exclamatory sentence.
2. After a very strong interjection.
3. At the end of an imperative sentence that exclaims.

A **comma** is used:
1. To separate items in a series.
2. To separate adjectives of equal value.
3. To separate a direct quotation from the rest of a sentence.
4. To separate the day of the month from the year.
5. To separate the names of a city and a state.
6. To separate a name from a title (*David Bird, President*).
7. To set off adjectives in an appositive position.
8. To set off introductory words like *no* and *now*.
9. To set off words like *however, moreover, too*.
10. To set off a name used in direct address.
11. To set off a nonrestrictive adjective clause.
12. To set off most words used in apposition.
13. After the greeting in a friendly letter.
14. After the closing in any letter.
15. After a last name preceding a first name.
16. After a mild interjection within a sentence.
17. After an introductory adverbial clause.
18. After an introductory participial phrase.
19. Before the conjunction in a compound sentence.
20. Whenever necessary to make meaning clear.

An **apostrophe** is used:
1. To show possession.
2. In contractions.
3. To form plurals of letters, figures, signs, and words.

Quotation marks are used:
1. To enclose the exact words of a speaker.
2. Around titles of short plays, short stories, short poems, chapter titles and songs.

A colon is used:
1. In writing time (*6:45*).
2. To introduce a list.
3. After the greeting in a business letter.
4. In written plays and in other forms of written dialogue, after the name of the character who is speaking.

A semicolon is used:
1. To join independent clauses in a compound sentence when a conjunction is not present.
2. To precede a conjunctive adverb (*therefore, however, furthermore,* etc.) used between the coordinate clauses of a compound sentence.
3. In place of a comma when a more distinct pause than that which a comma indicates is desired.

Underlining is used:
1. Below handwritten or typewritten titles of movies, newspapers, books, magazines, ships and trains.
2. To set off foreign words and phrases which are not yet part of the English language.

A hyphen is used:
1. In writing compound numbers.
2. To divide a word at the end of a line.
3. Between parts of a compound adjective preceding a noun.

A dash is used:
1. To indicate an abrupt break in thought or structure.
2. To indicate a parenthetical or explanatory phrase or clause.
3. Between numbers in a page reference.

Parentheses are used:
1. To enclose material that is supplementary, explanatory or interpretive.
2. To enclose a question mark after a date or a statement to show doubt.
3. To enclose an author's insertion or comment.

DICTIONARIES

The American Heritage Dictionary of the English Language
  W. Morris, ed. American Heritage Pub. Co./Houghton Mifflin

Bernstein's Reverse Dictionary
  Bernstein. The New York Times Book Co.

The Complete Rhyming Dictionary
  C. Wood, ed. Doubleday & Co.

Doublespeak Dictionary
  W. Lambdin. Pinnacle.

Macmillan Dictionary for Children
  P. R. Winant, sup. ed. Macmillan Pub. Co., Inc.

New Rhyming Dictionary and Poet's Handbook
  Johnson. Harper & Row.

Webster's New World Speller/Divider
  _____ . W. Collins, Pub.

Webster's Seventh New Collegiate Dictionary
  _____ . G. and C. Merriam Co.

GRAMMAR AND USAGE

The Art of Styling Sentences
  Waddell, Esch, and Walker. Barrons.

The Complete Letter Writer
  N. H. and S. K. Mager. Simon & Schuster.

The Golden Book on Writing
  Lambuth. Penguin.

Instant Vocabulary
  Ehrlich. Pocket Books.

Letters for All Occasions
  Myers. Barnes and Noble.

The New York Times Manual of Style and Usage
  L. Jordan, ed. Quadrangle/The New York Times Book Co.

Use the Right Word
  S. I. Hayakawa, ed. The Reader's Digest Assn., Inc.

Word Watcher's Handbook
  Martin. David McKay Co., Inc.

Write It Right
  Kredenser. Barnes and Noble.

The Written Word
  A. D. Steinhardt, sup. ed. Houghton Mifflin.

STUDY SKILLS BUILDERS
Dictionary Dynamite
   I. Forte and J. MacKenzie. Incentive Pub., Inc.
Fraction Action
   M. Frank. Incentive Pub., Inc.
Library Lingo
   S. Schurr. Incentive Pub., Inc.
Mainly Math
   S. Schurr. Incentive Pub., Inc.
Newspaper Know-How
   C. Farnette. Incentive Pub., Inc.
Study Skills Shop
   C. Farnette. Incentive Pub., Inc.
Think About It (Primary and Middle Grades Levels)
   I. Forte. Incentive Pub., Inc.

WORD USAGE
Bartlett's Familiar Quotations
   E. M. Beck, ed. Little, Brown & Co.
A Basic Dictionary of Synonyms and Antonyms
   L. Urdang. Elsevier/Nelson Books.
The Clear and Simple Thesaurus Dictionary
   Wittels and Greisman. Grosset and Dunlap.
Dictionary of American Slang
   Wentworth and Flexner. Simon and Schuster.
The International Thesaurus of Quotations
   R. T. Tripp, comp. Thomas Y. Crowell Co.
Roget's International Thesaurus, 3rd ed.
   _____ . Thomas Y. Crowell Co.
The Word Finder
   E. J. Fluck, et al. Rodale Press
Yellow Pages for Students and Teachers
   The KIDS' STUFF People. Incentive Pub., Inc.

ℛOMAN NUMERALS

Basic Components: I = 1; V = 5; X = 10; L = 50; C = 100; D = 500; M = 1,000.

Rules:
1) Only I can go before V or X (it reduces each by 1).
2) Only X can go before L or C (it reduces each by 10).
3) Only C can go before D or M (it reduces each by 100).
4) I can appear only 3 times after V.
5) X can appear only 3 times after L.
6) C can appear only 3 times after D or M.
7) The value of each symbol never changes.

1 = I	26 = XXVI	51 = LI	76 = LXXVI
2 = II	27 = XXVII	52 = LII	77 = LXXVII
3 = III	28 = XXVIII	53 = LIII	78 = LXXVIII
4 = IV	29 = XXIX	54 = LIV	79 = LXXIX
5 = V	30 = XXX	55 = LV	80 = LXXX
6 = VI	31 = XXXI	56 = LVI	81 = LXXXI
7 = VII	32 = XXXII	57 = LVII	82 = LXXXII
8 = VIII	33 = XXXIII	58 = LVIII	83 = LXXXIII
9 = IX	34 = XXXIV	59 = LIX	84 = LXXXIV
10 = X	35 = XXXV	60 = LX	85 = LXXXV
11 = XI	36 = XXXVI	61 = LXI	86 = LXXXVI
12 = XII	37 = XXXVII	62 = LXII	87 = LXXXVII
13 = XIII	38 = XXXVIII	63 = LXIII	88 = LXXXVIII
14 = XIV	39 = XXXIX	64 = LXIV	89 = LXXXIX
15 = XV	40 = XL	65 = LXV	90 = XC
16 = XVI	41 = XLI	66 = LXVI	91 = XCI
17 = XVII	42 = XLII	67 = LXVII	92 = XCII
18 = XVIII	43 = XLIII	68 = LXVIII	93 = XCIII
19 = XIX	44 = XLIV	69 = LXIX	94 = XCIV
20 = XX	45 = XLV	70 = LXX	95 = XCV
21 = XXI	46 = XLVI	71 = LXXI	96 = XCVI
22 = XXII	47 = XLVII	72 = LXXII	97 = XCVII
23 = XXIII	48 = XLVIII	73 = LXXIII	98 = XCVIII
24 = XXIV	49 = XLIX	74 = LXXIV	99 = XCIX
25 = XXV	50 = L	75 = LXXV	100 = C

OTHER EXAMPLES:

101 = CI
204 = CCIV
323 = CCCXXIII
400 = CD
499 = CDXCIX
502 = DII

610 = DCX
734 = DCCXXXIV
870 = DCCCLXX
900 = CM
962 = CMLXII
1,203 = MCCIII

wish	**dream**	**boy**	**girl**
dish	cream	coy	curl
fish	gleam	enjoy	hurl
squish	team	joy	swirl
swish	steam	toy	twirl

match	**love**	**miss**	**ten**
catch	dove	bliss	been
hatch	glove	hiss	den
latch	of	kiss	hen
patch	shove	this	men

cat	**bunk**	**ball**	**weak**
bat	clunk	call	beak
fat	dunk	crawl	cheek
flat	drunk	fall	leak
hat	hunk	gall	meek
mat	junk	hall	peak
pat	punk	mall	peek
rat	sunk	stall	reek
sat	stunk	tall	seek
slat	trunk	wall	week

think	**rain**	**and**	**bare**
blink	cane	band	bear
brink	gain	brand	care
clink	lain	canned	dare
drink	main	fanned	fare
link	pain	gland	hair
pink	pane	grand	pear
rink	stain	hand	rare
sink	train	land	stare
wink	vain	sand	there

black	**block**	**blue**	**date**
back	clock	clue	ate
crack	cock	crew	bait
lack	dock	drew	fate
pack	flock	few	gate
quack	knock	flew	hate
rack	lock	glue	late
sack	mock	knew	mate
smack	rock	new	rate
stack	sock	to	state

(cont.)

friend	**gold**	**tone**	**snow**
bend	bold	bone	blow
blend	bowled	cone	crow
end	cold	groan	flow
lend	fold	known	go
mend	hold	lone	know
pretend	mold	moan	low
rend	old	phone	mow
send	rolled	stone	no
spend	sold	thrown	row
tend	told	zone	so

book	**burn**	**time**	**fist**
brook	churn	crime	grist
cook	earn	dime	hissed
crook	learn	grime	kissed
hook	stern	lime	list
look	turn	rhyme	mist
took	yearn	slime	twist

day	**dear**	**eye**	**four**
clay	deer	by	core
gay	fear	cry	door
hay	hear	fry	floor
lay	here	high	more
may	near	I	pour
play	peer	lie	roar
ray	queer	pie	sore
say	rear	sigh	store
tray	steer	tie	tore
way	year	why	wore

bowl	**man**	**grade**	**green**
coal	ban	ade	bean
foal	can	blade	clean
goal	fan	fade	dean
hole	pan	glade	glean
mole	plan	laid	keen
pole	ran	made	lean
roll	tan	maid	mean
soul	van	paid	queen

map	**night**	**nine**	**ring**
cap	bite	dine	bring
clap	bright	fine	cling
flap	fight	line	ding
gap	kite	mine	fling
lap	light	pine	king
nap	quite	sign	sing
slap	right	swine	sling
tap	sight	tine	sting
trap	tight	vine	swing
wrap	white	whine	wing

room	**run**	**tale**	**three**
boom	bun	dale	be
bloom	done	fail	flea
broom	fun	gale	glee
doom	gun	hale	key
fume	none	jail	knee
gloom	one	male	me
groom	pun	nail	see
loom	sun	pale	tea
tomb	ton	rail	tree
zoom	won	sale	we

bog	**thought**	**star**	**tin**
cog	bought	are	bin
fog	brought	bar	din
flog	caught	car	fin
frog	fought	far	gin
hog	ought	jar	kin
jog	sought	mar	pin
log	taught	tar	sin
smog	taut	war	win

five	**six**
chive	fix
dive	kicks
drive	licks
hive	picks
jive	sticks
live	ticks

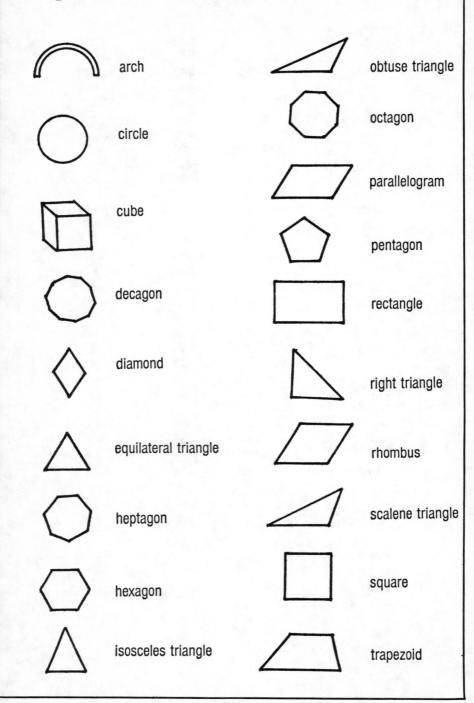

arch

obtuse triangle

circle

octagon

cube

parallelogram

decagon

pentagon

diamond

rectangle

equilateral triangle

right triangle

heptagon

rhombus

hexagon

scalene triangle

isosceles triangle

square

trapezoid

SIMILES

A simile is a comparison of two basically unlike things introduced by like or as.

My love is like a red, red rose. (Burns)
Things look about as hopeless as a frost in spring. (Tolkien)
We are such stuff as dreams are made on.... (Shakespeare)
My heart is true as steel.... (Shakespeare)
Her pretty feet, like snails, did creep/A little out.... (Herrick)
Our hopes, like towering falcons, aim at objects in an airy height.
   (Prior)
Therefore my age is as a lusty winter, frosty but kindly.
   (Shakespeare)
Joy rises in me, like a summer's morn. (Coleridge)
She walks in beauty, like the night/Of cloudless climes and
   starry skies. (Byron)
She sat like Patience on a monument, smiling at grief.
   (Shakespeare)
The Assyrian came down like the wolf on the fold. (Byron)
But he lay like a warrior taking his rest.... (Wolfe)
Life, like a dome of many-colored glass, stains the white
   radiance of eternity. (Shelley)
Suddenly a thought came like a full-blown rose/FLushing his
   brow. (Keats)
Silence is deep as Eternity; Speech is shallow as Time. (Carlyle)

SYNONYMS, ANTONYMS and HOMONYMS

Word	Synonym	Antonym	Homonym
aid	help	hinder	ade, aide
air	atmosphere	earth	heir
aisle	passageway	blockade	isle
all	everything	none	awl
alter	change	preserve	altar
ate	consumed	fasted	eight
bare	naked	clothed	bear
basis	foundation	summit	bases
be	exist	isn't	bee
beach	shore	ocean	beech
been	was	wasn't	bin
blew	gusted	calmed	blue
bore	weary	excite	boar

(cont.)

Word	Synonym	Antonym	Homonym
bow*	submit	refuse	bough
break	shatter	repair	brake
bridle	curb	free	bridal
bury	inter	unearth	berry
buy	purchase	sell	by, bye
capital	wealth	liability	capitol
caret	insertion	deletion	carot, carrot
coarse	rough	smooth	course
compliment	praise	criticise	complement
counsel	advise	ignore	council
dear	expensive	cheap	deer
desert*	abandon	retrieve	dessert
die	decease	live	dye
disperse	distribute	gather	disburse
elusive	evasive	overt	illusive
eminent	prominent	obscure	imminent
fair	just	unfair	fare
flower	bloom	die	flour
forth	forward	back	fourth
formerly	before	after	formally
great	large	small	grate
groan	moan	laugh	grown
heal	cure	infect	heel
here	present	there	hear
heroine	victor	loser	heroin
holy	sacred	profane	wholly
idle	slothful	busy	idol, idyll
illusive	phantasmal	tangible	elusive
in	inside	out	inn
iniquity	wickedness	goodness	inequity
knave	rascal	gentleman	nave
knows	understands	(is) ignorant	nose
leave	depart	return	leaf
led	guided	followed	lead*
lone	one	several	loan
low	inferior	high	lo
made	created	destroyed	maid
male	man	woman	mail
meet	assemble	adjourn	meat

*heteronym

Word	Synonym	Antonym	Homonym
minor	petty	major	miner
mourning	grief	gladness	morning
muscle	strength	weakness	mussel
need	require	have	knead
new	contemporary	old	knew, gnu
night	evening	day	knight
no	negative	yes	know
none	nothing	all	nun
pain	ache	pleasure	pane
pair	twins	single	pare
pale	pallid	rosy	pail
peace	accord	war	piece
place	put	remove	plaice
plain	intelligible	confusing	plane
presence	proximity	absence	presents*
prey	quarry	hunter	pray
principle	essential	unnecessary	principal
raise	elevate	lower	raze
real	actual	fake	reel
red	florid	pale	read*
reign	rule	obey	rain
right	correct	wrong	wright, rite
rode	drove	walked	road
rough	coarse	smooth	ruff
rumor	gossip	truth	roomer
seem	appear	is	seam
sell	vend	purchase	cell
sent	dispatched	returned	scent, cent
serf	slave	master	surf
sheer	thin	opaque	shear
sight	vision	blindness	site, cite
slay	murder	save	sleigh
slow	dilatory	fast	sloe
soar	fly	land	sore
sole	only	several	soul
some	few	many	sum
son	scion	daughter	sun
sow*	plant	reap	so, sew
stare	gaze	glance	stair

*heteronym

(cont.)

SYNONYMS, ANTONYMS and HOMONYMS (cont.)

stationary	motionless	movable	stationery
steal	rob	buy	steel
straight	undeviating	curved	strait
taught	instructed	learned	taut
threw	pitched	caught	through
tow	pull	push	toe
vain	futile	warranted	vein, vane
vice	fault	virtue	vise
wait	tarry	rush	weight
want	desire	need	wont
waste	squander	conserve	waist
weak	feeble	strong	week
whoa	stop	go	woe
won	succeeded	lost	one
wry	crooked	straight	rye

*heteronym

𝕋ABLES OF MEASUREMENT

Metric   *English*

LENGTH

Metric	English
1 centimeter (cm) = 10 millimeters (mm)	1 foot (ft.) = 12 inches (in.)
1 decimeter (dm) = 10 centimeters	1 yard (yd.) = 36 inches
1 meter (m) = 10 decimeters	1 yard = 3 feet
1 meter = 100 centimeters	1 rod (rd.) = 16½ feet
1 decameter (dkm) = 10 meters	1 mile (mi.) = 5,280 feet
1 kilometer (km) = 1000 meters	1 mile = 1,760 yards

WEIGHT

Metric	English
1 gram (gr) = 1000 milligrams (mg)	1 pound (lb.) = 16 ounces (oz.)
1 kilogram (kg) = 1000 grams	1 ton = 2000 pounds
1 metric ton = 1000 kilograms	

CAPACITY

Metric	English
1 liter (1) = 1000 milliliters (ml)	1 pint (pt.) = 2 cups
1 decaliter (dkl) = 10 liters	1 quart (qt.) = 2 pints
1 kiloliter (kl) = 1000 liters	1 gallon (gal.) = 4 quarts
	1 peck (pk.) = 8 quarts
	1 bushel (bu.) = 4 pecks

TEMPERATURE CONVERSION SCALE

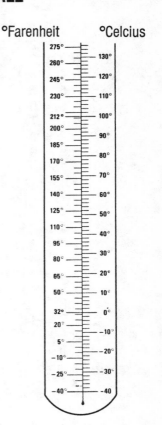

°Farenheit   °Celcius

32° Fahrenheit = 0° Celsius
0° Fahrenheit = -17.8° Celsius

Water boils at 100 degrees
   Celsius; 212 degrees
   Farenheit.

Normal body temperature is
   37 degrees Celcius;
   98.6 degrees Farenheit.

Water freezes at 0 degrees
   Cecius; 32 degrees Farenheit.

TIME

1 minute (min.)	= 60 seconds (sec.)
1 hour (hr.)	= 60 minutes
1 day	= 24 hours
1 week	= 7 days
1 month	= 28, 29, 30 or 31 days
1 year	= 52 weeks
1 year	= 365 or 366 days
1 year	= 12 months
1 decade	= 10 years
1 century	= 100 years

TIMES TABLES

1 x 1 = 1	4 x 1 = 4
1 x 2 = 2	4 x 2 = 8
1 x 3 = 3	4 x 3 = 12
1 x 4 = 4	4 x 4 = 16
1 x 5 = 5	4 x 5 = 20
1 x 6 = 6	4 x 6 = 24
1 x 7 = 7	4 x 7 = 28
1 x 8 = 8	4 x 8 = 32
1 x 9 = 9	4 x 9 = 36
1 x 10 = 10	4 x 10 = 40
1 x 11 = 11	4 x 11 = 44
1 x 12 = 12	4 x 12 = 48
2 x 1 = 2	5 x 1 = 5
2 x 2 = 4	5 x 2 = 10
2 x 3 = 6	5 x 3 = 15
2 x 4 = 8	5 x 4 = 20
2 x 5 = 10	5 x 5 = 25
2 x 6 = 12	5 x 6 = 30
2 x 7 = 14	5 x 7 = 35
2 x 8 = 16	5 x 8 = 40
2 x 9 = 18	5 x 9 = 45
2 x 10 = 20	5 x 10 = 50
2 x 11 = 22	5 x 11 = 55
2 x 12 = 24	5 x 12 = 60
3 x 1 = 3	6 x 1 = 6
3 x 2 = 6	6 x 2 = 12
3 x 3 = 9	6 x 3 = 18
3 x 4 = 12	6 x 4 = 24
3 x 5 = 15	6 x 5 = 30
3 x 6 = 18	6 x 6 = 36
3 x 7 = 21	6 x 7 = 42
3 x 8 = 24	6 x 8 = 48
3 x 9 = 27	6 x 9 = 54
3 x 10 = 30	6 x 10 = 60
3 x 11 = 33	6 x 11 = 66
3 x 12 = 36	6 x 12 = 72

7 x 1 = 7	10 x 1 = 10
7 x 2 = 14	10 x 2 = 20
7 x 3 = 21	10 x 3 = 30
7 x 4 = 28	10 x 4 = 40
7 x 5 = 35	10 x 5 = 50
7 x 6 = 42	10 x 6 = 60
7 x 7 = 49	10 x 7 = 70
7 x 8 = 56	10 x 8 = 80
7 x 9 = 63	10 x 9 = 90
7 x 10 = 70	10 x 10 = 100
7 x 11 = 77	10 x 11 = 110
7 x 12 = 84	10 x 12 = 120
8 x 1 = 8	11 x 1 = 11
8 x 2 = 16	11 x 2 = 22
8 x 3 = 24	11 x 3 = 33
8 x 4 = 32	11 x 4 = 44
8 x 5 = 40	11 x 5 = 55
8 x 6 = 48	11 x 6 = 66
8 x 7 = 56	11 x 7 = 77
8 x 8 = 64	11 x 8 = 88
8 x 9 = 72	11 x 9 = 99
8 x 10 = 80	11 x 10 = 110
8 x 11 = 88	11 x 11 = 121
8 x 12 = 96	11 x 12 = 132
9 x 1 = 9	12 x 1 = 12
9 x 2 = 18	12 x 2 = 24
9 x 3 = 27	12 x 3 = 36
9 x 4 = 36	12 x 4 = 48
9 x 5 = 45	12 x 5 = 60
9 x 6 = 54	12 x 6 = 72
9 x 7 = 63	12 x 7 = 84
9 x 8 = 72	12 x 8 = 96
9 x 9 = 81	12 x 9 = 108
9 x 10 = 90	12 x 10 = 120
9 x 11 = 99	12 x 11 = 132
9 x 12 = 108	12 x 12 = 144

ads (for magazines, newspapers, yellow pages)
advice columns
allegories
anecdotes
announcements
anthems
appendices
apologies
assumptions
autobiographies
awards
ballads
beauty tips
bedtime stories
beginnings
billboards
biographies
blurbs
books
book jackets
book reviews
brochures
bulletins
bumper stickers
calendar quips
calorie charts
campaign speeches
captions
cartoons
cereal boxes
certificates
character sketches
comic strips
community bulletins
comparisons
complaints
constitutions
contracts
conundrums
conversations

couplets
critiques
cumulative stories
data sheets
definitions
descriptions
diaries
diets
directions
directories
documents
doubletalk
dramas
dream scripts
editorials
encyclopedia entries
epilogues
epitaphs
endings
essays
evaluations
exaggerations
exclamations
explanations
fables
fairy tales
fantasies
fashion articles
fashion show scripts
folklore
fortunes
game rules
graffiti
good news-bad news
greeting cards
grocery lists
gossip
headlines
horoscopes
how-to-do-it speeches
impromptu speeches
indexes

inquiries
insults
interviews
introductions
invitations
job applications
jokes
journals
jump rope rhymes
knock-knock jokes
labels
legends
letters
lies
lists
love notes
luscious words
lyrics
magazines
marquee notices
memories
metaphors
menus
monologues
movie reviews
movie scripts
mysteries
myths
news analyses
newscasts
newspapers
nonsense
nursery rhymes
obituaries
observations
odes
opinions
palindromes
pamphlets
parodies
party tips
persuasive letters

phrases
plays
poems
post cards
posters
prayers
problems
proformas
profound sayings
prologues
proposals
propaganda sheets
protest signs
protest letters
product descriptions
proverbs
puppet shows
puns
puzzles
quips
quizzes
questionnaires
questions
quotations
ransom notes
reactions
real estate notices
rebuttals
recipes
record covers

remedies
reports
requests
requiems
requisitions
resumes
reviews
revisions
riddles
sale notices
sales pitches
satires
schedules
secrets
self descriptions
sentences
sequels
serialized stories
sermons
signs
silly sayings
skywriting messages
slogans
soap operas
society news
solutions
songs
speeches
spoofs
spoonerisms

sports analyses
superstitions
TV commercials
TV guides
TV programs
tall tales
telegrams
telephone directories
textbooks
thank you notes
theater programs
titles
tongue twisters
traffic rules
transcripts
travel folders
travel posters
tributes
trivia
used car descriptions
vignettes
want ads
wanted posters
warnings
wills
wise sayings
wishes
weather reports
weather forecasts
yarns

From: IF YOU'RE TRYING TO TEACH KIDS HOW TO WRITE, YOU'VE GOTTA HAVE THIS BOOK! by Marge Frank.
Copyright © 1979 by Incentive Publications, Inc. Used by permission.

THINGS TO WRITE ABOUT

Famous people
School
When you were sick
Your hero or heroine
Friends
Pets
Holidays
Yourself
Romance
Death
Events in your life
Times when you were brave
Your home
History
Colors
Your favorite TV show
Health care
Your country
Hungry times
Your own special place
Quiet times
School
Your favorite piece of clothing
Secrets
Ethics
Challenges
What you believe
Politics
Depression
Things you hate
Weather
Fantasies

Your favorite movie
Vacations
Feelings
Times when you were afraid
Thoughts
Foods
Books
Pain
Family
Nature
Make-believe worlds
Scientific discoveries
Outer space
Your community
Art
Disasters
Wars
Sports events
Feeling safe
Bad things you have done
What you wish your parents
    understood
Fads
Crafts
Teachers
Things you're thankful for
Rainbows
Stars
Ways to make money
Your favorite game
Wishes
Careers
... and YOUR OWN ideas!

ability (power), **capacity** (condition)
accede (agree), **exceed** (surpass)
accept (receive), **except** (exclude)
adapt (adjust), **adopt** (accept)
advise (to give advice), **advice** (counsel or recommendation)
affect (to influence), **effect** (result)
all ready (completely prepared), **already** (previously)
allude (refer to), **elude** (escape)
allusion (reference), **illusion** (false perception), **delusion** (false belief)
assure (to set a person's mind at ease), **insure** (guarantee life or property against harm), **ensure** (to secure from harm)
avenge (to achieve justice), **revenge** (retaliation)
averse (opposition on the subject's part), **adverse** (opposition against the subject's will)
avoid (shun), **prevent** (thwart), **avert** (turn away)
between (use when referring to two persons, places or things), **among** (use when referring to more than two places, persons, or things)
capital (seat of government), **capitol** (building)
censor (one who prohibits offensive material), **censure** (to criticize)
cite (to bring forward as support or truth), **quote** (to repeat exactly)
clench (to grip something tightly, as hand or teeth), **clinch** (to secure a bargain or something abstract)
complement (something that completes), **compliment** (an expression of praise)
compromise (a settlement in which each side makes concession), **surrender** (to yield completely)
confidant (one to whom secrets are told), **confidante** (a female confidant), **confident** (assured of success)
constant (unchanging), **continual** (repeated regularly), **continuous** (action without interruption)
contagious (transmissable by contact), **infectious** (capable of causing infection)
consul (a country's representative in a foreign country), **council** (a deliberative assembly), **councilor** (member of a deliberative body), **counsel** (to give advice), **counselor** (one who gives advice)
credible (plausible), **creditable** (deserving commendation), **credulous** (gullible)

(cont.)

deny (contradict), **refute** (to give evidence to disprove something) **repudiate** (to reject the validity of)

doubtless (presumption of certainty), **undoubtedly** (definite certainty)

elegy (a mournful poem), **eulogy** (a speech honoring a deceased person)

element (a basic assumption), **factor** (something that contributes to a result)

elicit (to evoke), **illicit** (unlawful)

emigrate (a single move by persons, used with *from*), **immigrate** (a single move by persons, used with *to*), **migrate** (seasonal movement)

eminent (prominent), **imminent** (soon to occur)

farther (literal distance), **further** (figurative distance)

fatal (causing death), **fateful** (affecting one's destiny)

feasible (clearly possible), **possible** (capable of happening)

fewer (refers to units capable of being individually counted), **less** (refers to collective quantities or to abstracts)

graceful (refers to movement), **gracious** (courteous)

impassable (impossible to traverse), **impassive** (devoid of emotion)

imply (to hint or suggest), **infer** (to draw conclusions based on facts)

incredible (unbelievable), **incredulous** (skeptical)

insignificant (trivial), **tiny** (small)

insinuate (to hint covertly), **intimate** (to imply subtly)

invoke (to call upon a higher power for assistance), **evoke** (to rewaken or inspire)

judicial (pertaining to law), **judicious** (exhibiting sound judgment)

latter (the second of two things mentioned), **later** (subsequently)

lay (to put or place), **lie** (to recline)

likely (use when mere probability is involved), **apt** (use when a known tendency is involved)

mania (craze), **phobia** (fear)

may (use when strong sense of permission or possibility is involved), **might** (use when weak sense of permission or possibility is involved)

mutual (refers to intangibles of a personal nature between two parties), **reciprocal** (refers to a balanced relationship in which one action is made on account of or in return for another)

nauseated (to feel queasy), **nauseous** (causing queasiness)

oblige (to feel a debt of gratitude), **obligate** (under direct compulsion to follow a certain course)

official (authorized by a proper authority), **officious** (extremely eager to offer help or advice)

older (refers to persons and things), **elder** (refers only to persons)

on (used to indicate motion to a position), **onto** (very strongly conveys motion toward), **on to** (use when *on* is an adverb and *to* is a preposition)

oral (refers to the sense of "word of mouth;" cannot refer to written words), **verbal** (can refer to both written and spoken words)

partly (use when stress is placed on a part in contrast to the whole), **partially** (use when the whole is stressed, often indirectly)

people (refers to a large group of individuals considered collectively), **persons** (refers to a small, specific number), **public** (a group of people sharing a common interest)

persecute (to oppress or harass), **prosecute** (to initiate legal or criminal action against)

piteous (pathetic), **pitiable** (lamentable), **pitiful** (very inferior or insignificant)

practically (almost), **virtually** (to all intents)

precipitant (rash, impulsive), **precipitate** (to hurl downward), **precipitous** (extremely steep)

principal (chief), **principle** (basic law or truth)

quite (very), **quiet** (hushed)

rack (a framework; to be in great pain), **wrack** (destruction by violent means)

raise (to move upward; to build; to breed), **rear** (to bring up a child), **rise** (to ascend)

rare (refers to unusual value and quality of which there is a permanent small supply), **scarce** (refers to temporary infrequency)

ravage (to devastate or despoil), **ravish** (to take away by force; to rape)

recourse (an application to something for aid or support), **resource** (an available supply)

regretful (sorrowful), **regrettable** (something that elicits mental distress)

reluctant (unwilling), **reticent** (refers to a temperament or style that is characteristically silent or restrained)

repel (drive off; cause distaste or aversion), **repulse** (drive off; reject by means of discourtesy)

respectfully (showing honor and esteem), **respectively** (one at a time in order)

(cont.)

restive (resistance to control), **restless** (lacking repose)

seasonal (refers to what applies to or depends on a season), **seasonable** (refers to timeliness or appropriateness to a season)

sensual (used when referring to the gratification of physical [sexual] senses), **sensuous** (usually refers to senses involved in aesthetic gratification)

sit (to rest the body on the buttocks with the torso upright; usually intransitive), **set** (to put or place something; usually transitive)

specific (explicitly set forth), **particular** (not general or universal)

stationary (immovable), **stationery** (matched writing paper and envelopes)

tasteful (exhibiting that which is proper or seemly in a social setting), **tasty** (having a pleasing flavor)

transient (refers to what literally stays for only a short time), **transitory** (short-lived, impermanent)

turbid (muddy, dense; in turmoil), **turgid** (swollen; grandiloquent)

weather (state of the atmosphere), **whether** (an indirect question involving alternatives)

From: THE YELLOW PAGES FOR STUDENTS & TEACHERS by the KIDS' STUFF People. Copyright © 1979 by Incentive Publications, Inc. Used by permission.

YOUR LIST